Lace Knitting

A selection of 26 patterns

SARIE VAN SCHALKWYK

CAPE TOWN

Acknowledgements

*The publishers acknowledge with thanks the kind coope-
ration of* Binnehuis Interiors *in providing the venue for the
photography and the accessories for styling.*

*J & P Coats for providing the crochet cotton used for the ar-
ticles in this book and for granting permission to publish
the pattern for the round tablecloth, centrepiece and doily
which appears on p. 32.*

*Annien Teubes for styling accessories for the photographs
on pp. 9 and 10.*

Kay's Haberdashery, Bellville for the circular knitting needles

© 1991 Delos
40 Heerengracht, Cape Town

Also available in Afrikaans as *Kantbrei – 'n Keur van 26 patrone*

Photography by Anton de Beer
Cover design by Etienne van Duyker
Typography by Debbie Odendaal
Typeset in 10 on 12 pt Helvetica by Unifoto, Cape Town
Printed and bound by Printkor, Cape Town

First edition, first impression 1991

ISBN 1-86826-180-8

Contents

Abbreviations

Knitting abbreviations

alt	alternative
beg	begin(ning)
dec	decrease
foll	following
k	knit
p	purl
psso	pass slipped stitch over
rep	repeat(s)
rnd(s)	round(s)
sl	slip
st(s)	stitch(es)
tbl	through back of loop
tog	together
yfd	yarn forward (to make a stitch Example: (k1, yfd, k1) = Knit 1 stitch so that yarn is at the back of the needle. Take yarn under needle to front and knit next stitch.
yon	yarn over needle (to make a stitch between a purl stitch and a knit stitch) Example: (p1, yon, k1) = Purl 1 stitch so that yarn is in front of needle, take yarn over needle to the back and knit next stitch.
yrn	yarn round needle (to make a stitch between a knit stitch and a purl stitch) Example 1: (k1, yrn, p1) = Knit 1 stitch so that yarn is at the back of the needle. Take yarn under needle to front, over needle to back and under needle to front again and purl next stitch. Example 2: (k1, yrn twice, k1) = Knit 1 stitch so that yarn is at back of needle, take yarn under needle to front, over needle to back and under needle to front again and over needle to back and knit the next stitch (to make 2 stitches).

Crochet abbreviations

ch	chain
dc	double crochet
ss	slip stitch
st(s)	stitch(es)
tr	treble

Introduction

Technique

In lace knitting the same basic stitches are used as in conventional knitting. What distinguishes lace knitting is that one usually knits in rounds, that is, from the centre towards the outer edge, and that crochet cotton is used instead of wool. The cotton yarn helps to create the characteristic lacey appearance in articles knitted in this manner. Lace knitting requires considerable concentration, patience and time. It is therefore worth using the best quality yarn. The articles in this book have all been knitted with pure cotton yarn. Synthetic crochet yarn is considerably cheaper and can also be used, but the quality is not the same.

When knitting a round article one usually uses four double-pointed needles: three containing the stitches that have been cast on and a fourth to knit with. Square or rectangular items usually require five double-pointed needles: four for the stitches and the fifth to knit with. This is, however, not a hard and fast rule. The number of needles used can vary according to the number of stitches originally cast on. Except in the case of very small items (such as saucer doilies), 30 cm double-pointed needles are usually the most comfortable to knit with. Use corks secured on the tips of the needles to prevent stitches from slipping off. Change to a circular needle when there are too many stitches for double-pointed needles. The length of the circular needle to be used is specified in the pattern.

2,50 mm needles were used for most of the items in this book as both double-pointed and circular needles are readily available in this size. Thinner needles can be used for a finer, and thicker needles for a coarser effect. Remember that the size of the needles and the thickness of the yarn affects the size of the item as well as the amount of yarn that will be required. The tension of the knitting also affects the measurements. The tension is correct when the stitches can easily be knitted off the needles but the needles do not slip out of the knitting. No. 5 and no. 8 crochet cotton was used for all the designs in this book as this yarn is particularly suitable for lace knitting and therefore produces the best results. White and ecru are the colours used most frequently, but the choice of colours is, of course, a matter of personal preference.

When knitting in rounds the right side of the work always faces the knitter. The yarn is fed from the needle on the right (if you are right-handed) and the stitches are knitted from the needle on the left. Instructions are usually only given for pattern rounds, therefore every alternate round, for which no instructions are given, is knitted plain (k). When knitting with two needles the right side and the wrong side of the work alternately faces the knitter. All the rows for which no instructions are given are knitted purl (p), unless otherwise stated.

Casting on

For articles knitted with two needles, the casting on is the same as for any other knitting technique. Where one starts at the centre of an article and knits towards the outer edge, either of the following methods can be used for casting on.

With knitting needles

Cast on the number of stitches specified in the pattern as for ordinary knitting and leave a yarn end of about 10 cm. Divide the stitches onto three or four needles as the pattern may require. Thread the yarn end through a darning needle. Form a circle with the knitting needles and join the two ends by sewing a few overcast stitches through the lower part of the first stitch on the first needle and the last stitch on the last needle. Leave the yarn end to be worked away later. Now knit as many rounds plain as specified by the pattern before starting on the pattern rounds.

With a crochet hook

Stitches can also be cast on using a crochet hook. Crochet four or more chain stitches and join them into a ring with a slip stitch. Then crochet as many double crochet into this ring as the number of stitches you are required to cast on and join with a slip stitch into the first double crochet. Transfer the loop remaining on the crochet hook onto a double-pointed knitting needle, pick up the stitches and knit one stitch into each double crochet, dividing the stitches onto three or four needles. Count this as the first knitted round and continue knitting according to the pattern.

Following the pattern

Read through the whole pattern before you start knitting and make sure that all the abbreviations and other instructions are clear. General abbreviations that are used in all the patterns appear on p. 4. Abbreviations that are only used in specific patterns have been placed at the beginning of the relevant pattern. The abbreviation m1 = make one stitch is not always interpreted in the same manner. Please read each explanation accompanying it with care.

As lace knitting is very complicated, losing your place in

the pattern can have disastrous consequences. To prevent this happening, place a firm piece of white cardboard or paper below the line to be knitted and secure it with a paper clip so that it cannot move. Move it down once the line has been knitted. A row-counter can also be used or jot down the row/round numbers on a piece of paper and cross them off as each one is completed.

Marking rounds and pattern repeats

Mark the beginning of a round with a coloured thread that is sewn into the knitting. Place the thread between the first stitch on the left-hand needle and the last stitch on the right-hand needle end leave the end hanging at the back of the knitting. Move the thread as the knitting progresses from round to round.

Use a different colour thread to mark the beginning of each pattern repeat especially if there are a lot of repeats in a pattern as with a large tablecloth or the runner on p. 44. This enables one to check the number of stitches and to ensure that the pattern works out between repeats. It is always easier to trace a mistake this way than to unpick a whole round.

Transferring stitches

When a round commences with the instruction to transfer one (or more) stitches from left to right, the required number of stitches are knitted from the left-hand needle onto the right-hand needle and the new beginning of the round is marked between the first and last needle. The same number of stitches are slipped from the remaining two or three double-pointed needles onto the end of the previous needle. When knitting with a circular needle the stitches are only transferred from the left to the right-hand needle.

Where the pattern requires one (or more) stitches to be transferred from right to left at the beginning of a round, the required number of stitches are slipped from the right-hand needle onto the left-hand needle without being knitted. Mark the new beginning of the round and adjust the stitches on the other needles as well.

In this book the instruction to transfer stitches is accompanied by the instruction to mark the new beginning of the round and to adjust the stitches on the other needles as well, only where the transfer of stitches occurs for the first time in a pattern. Where stitches are transferred thereafter, the accompanying instructions are not repeated.

Pattern repeats

A complete pattern repeat is indicated by an asterisk at the beginning and the number of times the instructions are to be repeated at the end. A repeat within a pattern repeat is placed in round brackets, followed by the number of times the instructions in brackets are to be worked.

Example: * Yrn, (k2 tog, k1) twice, sl 1, k1, psso; rep from * to end. The instructions in brackets must be worked twice before the remaining instructions are continued and the instructions after the asterisk are repeated to the end of the round.

Where a repeat occurs within the repeat in round brackets, this repeat is placed in square brackets, followed by the number of times the instructions in square brackets must be worked.

Example: ([Yfd, k2 tog] 3 times, k2) 6 times. The instructions in square brackets [ ] are worked 3 times followed by k2. The instructions in round brackets ( ) are worked 6 times.

In complicated patterns such as that for the runner on p. 44, it can occur that a previous part of the pattern has to be knitted again within a pattern repeat. Such repeats are placed between one, two or even three asterisks with instructions to repeat the part from * to * or from ** to ** a certain number of times.

Should you find it difficult to follow a long and complicated round, it might be advisable to copy out the instructions and to write out the pattern repeats in full so that they are easier to follow.

Regularly count the stitches after each repeat to ensure that you have not made a mistake. Many patterns indicate the number of stitches at the end of each round and some also give the number of pattern repeats in each round.

When you interrupt your knitting, mark the place where you have stopped clearly on the pattern.

Joining the yarn

Joining yarn ends can be difficult in lace knitting due to the openwork character of the patterns. Try to place joins where they will be least visible. Leave a yarn end of about 10 cm and join the end of the new ball to this end with a single knot. Leave the ends on the wrong side of the knitting and knit a full round. Only when you have knitted past the join, should the knot be tightened and the yarn knotted a second time. The yarn ends are left to be worked into the back of the stitches at a later stage.

Handling the knitting

Take care not to leave knitting where it can be interfered with. Finding mistakes and unpicking stitches is extremely difficult in lace knitting. Keep your knitting and yarn in a bag to ensure that it remains clean and make sure that your hands are always clean and dry. Dusting your hands with a little talcum powder before you start knitting will promote the smoothe flow of the yarn.

Casting off

Most of the designs in this book are finished off with a simple crocheted edging. This does not require any particular knowledge of crocheting as only a few basic crochet stitches are used, viz. the double crochet, chain stitch and slip stitch.

Usually a group of three or four stitches is crocheted off the knitting needle as follows: Insert the crochet hook through the back of the stitches, take the yarn over the crochet hook and pull it through the knitted stitches, slip the stitches off the knitting needle and complete the double crochet. Now crochet a loop consisting of a number of chain stitches. The size of the loop is determined by the number of chain stitches. The loops should form round scallops and not lie tightly against the knitting. Adjust the number of chain stitches according to the manner in which you crochet. Use more chain stitches than the pattern indicates if you are inclined to crochet tightly and fewer if you crochet loosely. After completing the chain stitch loop another group of stitches is crocheted off the knitting needle with a double crochet and this is followed by another chain stitch loop. Work right round the article in this manner and join the last chain stitch to the first double crochet with a slip stitch.

If you cannot crochet, cast off as you would for ordinary knitting. Cast off loosely so that the edge does not pucker. Use a knitting needle one size larger than the one with which you have knitted if you are inclined to knit tightly. Leave a yarn end of about 10 cm when you have finished. Thread the yarn through a darning needle and work it through the back of the stitches on the wrong side of the knitting as unobtrusively as possible. Do not cut off the remaining end until the article has been rinsed, pinned out and left to dry. If preferred, the cast-off edge can be finished off with a knitted edging.

Washing and stretching knitting

Once it has been completed, lace knitting must be pinned out and stretched while it is damp to ensure a professional finish. Wash the article gently in lukewarm soap suds and rinse it thoroughly in clean water. If the item does not need to be washed it should still be rinsed in lukewarm water. Squeeze out most of the water and pin the article out to size with rust-proof pins on a flat surface. Start at the centre and work systematically towards the outer edge. Finish with a pin in each crocheted loop. Do not stretch the stitches excessively. Take care to pin out the crocheted loops or the cast-off edge evenly. To ensure that this is done, draw a circle or rectangle as large as that specified by the pattern on white paper and pin the article out along the outlines. Foamolite boards are extremely handy for pinning knitting on as the pins go into the boards easily. Large articles such as tablecloths are best pinned out on a clean sheet on a fitted carpet.

Leave the article until it is completely dry before removing the pins. If necessary knitting can be pressed by placing a clean white cloth over the wrong side of the article and ironing it lightly with a warm iron. Do not press too hard as this will give the knitting a flat, lifeless appearance. Items knitted with pure cotton yarn need not be pressed. Lace knitting has to be pinned out to size every time it is washed.

Lace knitting is relaxing, but as the patterns require considerable concentration it should not be attempted while watching television or making conversation. Enjoy knitting heirlooms for your family and special gifts for your friends.

Knitted lace edging

Lace edging for towel set

Materials

1 x 50 g Tridalia crochet cotton no. 5
One pair 2,50 mm knitting needles
Bath towel: 50 cm × 100 cm
Guest towel: 30 cm × 50 cm
Face cloth

Width of edging for bath towel: 4 cm

Instructions

Cast on 9 sts.
1st row: K4, (yfd, k2 tog) twice, yfd, k1.
2nd and every alt row: Knit.
3rd row: K5, (yfd, k2 tog) twice, yfd, k1.
5th row: K6, (yfd, k2 tog) twice, yfd, k1.
7th row: K7, (yfd, k2 tog) twice, yfd, k1.
9th row: K8, (yfd, k2 tog) twice, yfd, k1 (= 14 sts).
10th row: Cast off 5 sts, knit to end.

Repeat rows 1-10 to required length.

Cast off. Damp, pin out to measurements and leave to dry.
Sew neatly to edge of towel.

Width of edging for guest towel: 3 cm

Instructions

Cast on 7 sts.
Knit as for 4 cm edging, but start 1st, 3rd, 5th, 7th and 9th rows with 2 sts less. Thus 1st row: K2, (yfd, k2 tog) twice, yfd, k1.

Cast off. Damp, pin out to measurements and leave to dry.
Sew neatly to edge of towel.

Width of edging for face cloth: 1,5 cm

Instructions

Cast on 5 sts.
1st row: K1, yfd, k2 tog, yrn twice, k2.
2nd row: K2, (k1, p1) into "yrn twice" of previous rnd, k3.

3rd row: K1, yfd, k2 tog, k4.
4th row: Cast off 2 sts, k4.

Rep rows 1-4 to required length.

Cast off. Damp, pin out to measurements and leave to dry.
Sew neatly onto face cloth.

Blue decorative border for bath towel

Materials

1 x 50 g Tridalia crochet cotton no. 8
One pair 2,50 mm knitting needles
Bath towel: 50 cm × 100 cm

Width of decorative border: 4 cm

Abbreviations: m1 – make 1 stitch = p into front and back of next st

Instructions

Cast on 8 sts.
1st row: K5, yfd, k1, yfd, k2.
2nd row: P6, m1, k3.
3rd row: K4, p1, k2, yfd, k1, yfd, k3.
4th row: P8, m1, k4.
5th row: K4, p2, k3, yfd, k1, yfd, k4.
6th row: P10, m1, k5.
7th row: K4, p3, k4, yfd, k1, yfd, k5.
8th row: P12, m1, k6.
9th row: K4, p4, sl 1, k1, psso, k7, k2 tog, k1.
10th row: P10, m1, k7.
11th row: K4, p5, sl 1, k1, psso, k5, k2 tog, k1.
12th row: P8, m1, k2, p1, k5.
13th row: K4, p1, k1, p4, sl 1, k1, psso, k3, k2 tog, k1.
14th row: P6, m1, k3, p1, k5.
15th row: K4, p1, k1, p2 tog, p3 tog, sl 1, k1, psso, k1, k2 tog, k1.
16th row: K1, p3 tog, k2, p1, k5.
17th row: K4, p1, k1, p2 tog, k2 tog.
18th row: P3, k5.

Repeat rows 1-18 to required length.

Cast off. Damp, pin out to measurements and leave to dry.
Sew neatly onto towel.

Soap sachets

Pink soap sachet

Materials

Remnants of pink crochet cotton no. 5 or no. 8
One pair 2,50 mm knitting needles
9 mm wide satin ribbon: 25 cm

Size: Oblong sachet: 11 cm long; round sachet: 8 cm in diameter

Instructions

Cast on 41 sts.
1st row: K1, * yfd, sl 1, k2 tog, psso, yfd, k1; rep from * to end.
2nd row: Knit.

Repeat pattern 16 times for an oblong soap sachet and 10 times for a round one.

Cast off as follows: P1, (p2 tog) to end (= 21 sts).
Next row: K1, (k2 tog) to end (= 11 sts).

Cut yarn, leaving a 25 cm yarn end. Using a tapestry needle, thread end through stitches on knitting needle and slip stitches off. Tighten yarn and use the remainder to sew up the side seam. Thread a piece of ribbon through the 2nd row of holes, put the soap in the sachet, and tie the ribbon in a bow.

Any easy lace pattern can be used to knit soap sachets. Adjust the number of stitches and the length of the sachet to the size of the soap.

Blue soap sachet

Materials

Remnants of blue crochet cotton no. 5 or no. 8.
One pair 2,50 mm knitting needles
9 mm wide satin ribbon: 25 cm

Size: 8 cm in diameter

Instructions

Cast on 42 sts.
1st row: K1, * yrn, p4 tog; rep from * to last st, k1.
2nd row: K1, * k1, (k1, p1, k1) into "yrn" of previous rnd; rep from * to last st, k1.
3rd row: Knit.

Repeat pattern 10 times (or to required length). Cast off by knitting 2 tog for 2 rows.

Finish off as described above for pink soap sachet.

Place mat with matching coaster and doily

Materials

2 × 50 g Tridalia crochet cotton no. 5
5 double-pointed 2,50 mm knitting needles: 30 cm long
1,75 mm crochet hook

Size: Place mat: 28 cm × 40 cm; coaster: 15 cm × 15 cm; doily: each side 13,5 cm

Abbreviations: m1 – make 1 stitch = knit into front and back of next st

Place mat

Instructions

Cast on 76 sts, leaving a yarn end of about 20 cm for sewing up centre seam. Divide stitches onto 4 needles (34, 4, 34, 4). Form circle and knit 1 rnd. Mark beginning of round at 1st needle with a coloured thread and commence pattern.

1st rnd: *1st needle:* Yrn twice, k1 tbl, * yrn twice, sl 1, k1, psso, k2 tog; rep from * to last st, yrn twice, k1 tbl.
2nd needle: Yrn twice, k2 tog, yrn twice, sl 1, k1, psso.
3rd and 4th needles: As 1st and 2nd needles (= 38, 6, 38, 6 sts).

2nd and every alt rnd: Knit, but k1, p1 into each "yrn twice" of previous rnd. Work tbl all sts worked tbl in previous rnd. The pattern is given for the 1st needle. Work 2nd, 3rd and 4th needles as 1st. The number of sts on each needle is indicated in brackets at the end of each rnd.

3rd rnd: Transfer 1 st from left to right and mark new beg of rnd. Where sts are transferred at the beg of a rnd, remember to adjust sts on other needles as well. Yrn twice, k1 tbl, * yrn twice, sl 1, k1, psso, k2 tog; rep from * to last st, yrn twice, k1 tbl (= 42, 10, 42, 10 sts).

5th rnd: As 3rd rnd (= 46, 14, 46, 14 sts).

7th rnd: As 3rd rnd (= 50, 18, 50, 18 sts).

9th rnd: Transfer 1 st from left to right, k1 tbl, yfd, * sl 1, k1, psso, k2 tog, yrn twice; rep from * to last 5 sts, sl 1, k1, psso, k2 tog, yfd, k1 tbl (= 50, 18, 50, 18 sts).

11th rnd: * K2 tbl, yfd, sl 1, k1, psso, k1, (k2 tog, yrn twice, sl 1, k1, psso) twice, k1, k2 tog, yfd; rep from * to last 2 sts, k2 tbl (= 50, 18, 50, 18 sts).

13th rnd: K1 tbl, * (yfd, sl 1, k1, psso) 3 times, k2 tog, yrn twice, sl 1, k1, psso, (k2 tog, yfd) twice, k2 tog; rep from * to last st, yfd, k1 tbl (= 48, 18, 48, 18 sts).

15th rnd: K1 tbl, * yfd, k1 tbl, yfd, sl 1, k1, psso, yfd, k3 tog tbl, yrn twice, sl 1, k1, psso, k2 tog, yrn twice, k3 tog, yfd, k2

tog; rep from * to last 2 sts, (yfd, k1 tbl) twice (= 50, 20, 50, 20 sts).

17th rnd: K1 tbl, * (k1 tbl, yfd) twice, k1 tbl, sl 1, k1, psso, yfd, sl 1, k1, psso, k2 tog, yrn twice, sl 1, k1, psso, k2 tog, yfd, k2 tog; rep from * to last 4 sts, (k1 tbl, yfd) twice, k2 tbl (= 52, 22, 52, 22 sts).

19th rnd: K1 tbl, * k1 tbl, p1, yon, k1 tbl, yrn, p1, k1 tbl, sl 1, k1, psso, yfd, sl 1, k1, psso, k2, k2 tog, yfd, k2 tog; rep from * to last 6 sts, k1 tbl, p1, yon, k1 tbl, yrn, p1, k2 tbl (= 54, 24, 54, 24 sts).

20th and every alt rnd: As 2nd rnd, but p each p st from previous round.

21st rnd: K1 tbl, * k1 tbl, p2, yon, k1 tbl, yrn, p2, k1 tbl, sl 1, k1, psso, yfd, sl 1, k1, psso, k2 tog, yfd, k2 tog; rep from * to last 8 sts, k1 tbl, p2, yon, k1 tbl, yrn, p2, k2 tbl (= 56, 26, 56, 26 sts).

23rd rnd: K1 tbl, * yfd, k1 tbl, p2, (k1 tbl, yfd) twice, k1 tbl, p2, k1 tbl, yfd **, (sl 1, k2 tog, psso) twice; rep from * to last l0 sts, rep from * to ** once, k1 tbl (= 60, 30, 60, 30 sts).

25th rnd: Yrn twice, * sl 1, k1, psso, yfd, k1 tbl, p2, k1 tbl, k1, yfd, k1 tbl, yfd, k1, k1 tbl, p2, k1 tbl, yfd, k2 tog; rep from * to end (= 70, 36, 70, 36 sts).

26th rnd: As 20th rnd.

27th rnd: Transfer 1 st from left to right, k1 tbl, * yfd, sl 1, k1, psso, yfd, k1 tbl, p2, k2 tog tbl, k3, k2 tog, p2, k1 tbl, yfd, k2 tog; rep from * to last st, yfd, k1 tbl (= 67, 35, 67, 35 sts).

29th rnd: K1 tbl, * yfd, k1 tbl, yfd, sl 1, k1, psso, yfd, k1 tbl, p2, k2 tog tbl, k1, k2 tog, p2, k1 tbl, yfd, k2 tog; rep from * to last 2 sts, (yfd, k1 tbl) twice (= 69, 37, 69, 37 sts).

31st rnd: K1 tbl, * yfd, k3, yfd, sl 1, k1, psso, yfd, k1 tbl, p2, sl 1, k2 tog, psso, p2, k1 tbl, yfd, k2 tog; rep from * to last 4 sts, yfd, k3, yfd, k1 tbl (= 71, 39, 71, 39 sts).

33rd rnd: K1 tbl, * yfd, sl 1, k1, psso, k1, k2 tog, yfd, sl 1, k1, psso, yfd, k1 tbl, p2 tog, p1, p2 tog, k1 tbl, yfd, k2 tog; rep from * to last 6 sts, yfd, sl 1, k1, psso, k1, k2 tog, yfd, k1 tbl (= 63, 35, 63, 35 sts).

35th rnd: K1 tbl, * yfd, k1 tbl, yfd, sl 1, k2 tog, psso, yfd, k1 tbl, yfd **, sl 1, k1, psso, yfd, k1 tbl, p3 tog, k1 tbl, yfd, k2 tog; rep from * to last 6 sts, rep once from * to **, k1 tbl (= 65, 37, 65, 37 sts).

37th rnd: K1 tbl, * yfd, k3, yfd, k1 tbl, yfd, k3, yfd **, sl 1, k1, psso, yfd, sl 1, k2 tog, psso, yfd, k2 tog; rep from * to last 8 sts, rep once from * to **, k1 tbl (= 77, 45, 77, 45 sts).

39th rnd: K1 tbl, * yfd, sl 1, k1, psso, k1, k2 tog, yfd, m1, yfd, sl 1, k1, psso, k1, k2 tog, yfd **, sl 1, k1, psso, yfd, k3 tog; rep from * to last 12 sts, rep once from * to **, k1 tbl (= 74, 44, 74, 44 sts).

41st rnd: K1 tbl, * yfd, k1 tbl, yfd, sl 1, k2 tog, psso, yfd, k2 tog, yfd, sl 1, k1, psso, yfd, sl 1, k2 tog, psso, yfd, k1 tbl, yfd **, sl 1, k2 tog, psso; rep from * to last 13 sts, rep once from

* to **, k1 tbl, (= 71, 43, 71, 43 sts).

43rd rnd: K1 tbl, * yfd, k3, yfd, k1 tbl, k2 tog, yfd, m1, yfd, sl 1, k1, psso, k1 tbl, yfd, k3, yfd, k1 tbl; rep from * to end (= 96, 58, 96, 58 sts).

45th rnd: * K1 tbl, yfd, sl 1, k1, psso, k1, (k2 tog, yfd) twice, k1, k2 tbl, k1, (yfd, sl 1, k1, psso) twice, k1, k2 tog, yfd; rep from * to last st, k1 tbl (= 96, 58, 96, 58 sts).

47th rnd: (K1 tbl, yfd) twice, * sl 1, k2 tog, psso, (yfd, k2 tog) twice, yfd, k2 tbl, (yfd, sl 1, k1, psso) twice **, (yfd, sl 1, k2 tog, psso) twice, yfd; rep from * to last 18 sts; rep once from * to **, yfd, sl 1, k2 tog, psso, yfd, k1 tbl, yfd, k1 tbl (= 90, 56, 90, 56 sts).

49th rnd: * K1 tbl, yfd, k3, yfd, k1 tbl, (k2 tog, yfd) twice, k1, k2 tbl, k1, (yfd, sl 1, k1, psso) twice; rep from * to last 5 sts, k1 tbl, yfd, k3, yfd, k1 tbl (= 102, 64, 102, 64 sts).

51st rnd: K1 tbl, * yfd, sl 1, k1, psso, k1, (k2 tog, yfd) 3 times, k2 tog, k1 tbl, yfd, k1 tbl, (sl 1, k1, psso, yfd) twice, sl 1, k1, psso; rep from * to last 6 sts, yfd, sl 1, k1, psso, k1, k2 tog, yfd, k1 tbl (= 97, 61, 97, 61 sts).

53rd rnd: K1 tbl, yfd, k1 tbl, * yfd, sl 1, k2 tog, psso, (yfd, k2 tog) 3 times, k1 tbl, p1, k1 tbl, (sl 1, k1, psso, yfd) twice, sl 1, k1, psso; rep from * to last 5 sts, yfd, sl 1, k2 tog, psso, (yfd, k1 tbl) twice (= 89, 57, 89, 57 sts).

55th rnd: Yrn twice, k1 tbl, yfd, k3, yfd, k1 tbl, k2 tog, * (yfd, k2 tog) twice, k1 tbl, p1, k1 tbl, (sl 1, k1, psso, yfd) twice, sl 1, k1, psso **, yfd, k3 tog; rep from * to last 18 sts, rep once from * to **, k1 tbl, yfd, k3, yfd, k1 tbl (= 85, 57, 85, 57 sts).

56th rnd: As 20th rnd.

Knit 1 st and then crochet sts off as follows: 1 dc into next 2, ** 8 ch, 1 dc into next 5 sts, (8 ch, 1 dc into next 3 sts) 4 times, 8 ch, 1 dc into next 5 sts, * (8 ch, 1 dc into next 3 sts) 3 times, 8 ch, 1 dc into next 5 sts *; rep twice from * to *, (8 ch, 1 dc into next 3 sts) 4 times, 8 ch, 1 dc into next 5 sts, (8 ch, 1 dc into next 2 sts) twice; rep from ** along short side of place mat, working from * to * once only. Complete the remaining two sides in the same manner, ending with (8 ch, 1 dc into next 2 sts) once instead of twice, 8 ch, 1 ss into 1st dc.

Cut yarn and work in yarn end.

Fold place mat in half lengthwise, with right sides facing, and neatly sew up the opening in the centre using the yarn end left when casting on. Match pattern carefully. Damp, pin out to size and leave to dry.

Coaster

Instructions

Cast on 8 sts (2 sts on each of 4 needles). Form a circle and knit 1 rnd tbl. Now commence pattern. The number of sts given in brackets refers to each of the 4 needles.

1st rnd: * K1 tbl, yfd, k1 tbl; rep from * to end (= 3 sts).

2nd and every alt rnd: Knit, but work tbl all sts worked tbl in previous rnd.

3rd rnd: * (K1 tbl, yfd) twice, k1 tbl; rep from * to end (= 5 sts).

5th rnd: * K1 tbl, (k1 tbl, yfd) twice, k2 tbl; rep from * to end (= 7 sts).

7th rnd: * K2 tbl, p1, yon, k1 tbl, yrn, p1, k2 tbl; rep from * to end (= 9sts).

8th rnd: As 2nd rnd, but p each p st from previous rnd.

9th rnd: * K2 tbl, p2, yon, k1 tbl, yrn, p2, k2 tbl; rep from * to end (= 11 sts).

11th rnd: * K1 tbl, yfd, k1 tbl, p2, k1 tbl, (yfd, k1 tbl) twice, p2, k1 tbl, yfd, k1 tbl; rep from * to end (= 15 sts).

13th to 26th rnd: Foll instructions for place mat from 25th to 38th rnd.

13th rnd (= 19 sts); 15th rnd (= 19 sts); 17th rnd (= 21 sts); 19th rnd (= 23 sts); 21st rnd (= 21 sts); 23rd rnd (= 23 sts) and 25th rnd (= 29 sts).

27th rnd: * (K1 tbl, yfd, sl 1, k1, psso, k1, k2 tog, yfd) twice, sl 1, k1, psso, yfd, k3 tog, (yfd, sl 1, k1, psso, k1, k2 tog, yfd, k1 tbl) twice; rep from * to end (= 27 sts).

29th rnd: * (K1 tbl, yfd) twice, sl 1, k2 tog, psso, yfd, k3, yfd, (sl 1, k2 tog, psso, yfd, k1 tbl, yfd) twice, sl 1, k2 tog, psso, yfd, k3, yfd, sl 1, k2 tog, psso, (yfd, k1 tbl) twice; rep from * to end (= 29 sts).

31st rnd: K1 tbl, yfd, k3, yfd, k1 tbl, yfd, sl 1, k1, psso, k1, k2 tog, yfd, k1 tbl, yfd, (k3, yfd, k1 tbl, yfd) twice, sl 1, k1, psso, k1, k2 tog, yfd, k1 tbl, yfd, k3, yfd, k1 tbl (= 37 sts).

32nd rnd: Knit.

Crochet sts off as follows: 1 dc into next 2 sts, * (5 ch, 1 dc into next 3 sts) 11 times, (5 ch, 1 dc into next 2 sts) twice; rep from *, ending with (5 ch, 1 dc into next 2 sts) once instead of twice, 5 ch, 1 ss into 1st dc.

Cut yarn and work in yarn end. Damp, pin out to size and leave to dry.

Doily

This pattern can be adapted to knit an attractive five-sided doily. The floral pattern in the centre has five petals. Use the pattern for the coaster but cast on 10 sts instead of 8. Work rnds 1-32. The number of sts on each needle will differ from those given for the coaster.

Crochet sts off as for coaster.

Saucer doilies

Saucer doily with spiral motif

Materials

1 x 50 g Tridalia crochet cotton no. 8 (enough for 6 saucer doilies)
4 double-pointed 2,00 mm needles
1,25 mm crochet hook

Size: 9 cm in diameter

Instructions

Cast on 6 sts (2 on each of 3 needles). Form circle and knit 1st rnd.
2nd rnd: * Yfd, k1; rep from * to end.
3rd and every alt rnd: Knit.
4th rnd: * Yfd, k2; rep from * to end.
6th rnd: * Yfd, k3; rep from * to end.
8th rnd: * Yfd, k1, yfd, k3; rep from * to end.
10th rnd: * Yfd, k1, yfd, k5; rep from * to end.
12th rnd: * Yfd, k1, yfd, k1, yfd, k4, k2 tog; rep from * to end.
14th rnd: * Yfd, k1, yfd, k1, yfd, k6, k2 tog; rep from * to end.
15th rnd: * K10, k2 tog; rep from * to end.
16th rnd: * Yfd, k1, yfd, k1, yfd, k7, k2 tog; rep from * to end.
17th rnd: * K11, k2 tog; rep from * to end.
18th rnd: * Yfd, k1, yfd, k1, yfd, k8, k2 tog; rep from * to end.
19th rnd: * K12, k2 tog; rep from * to end.
20th rnd: * Yfd, k1, yfd, k1, yfd, k9, k2 tog; rep from * to end.
21st rnd: Knit.

Crochet sts off as follows: * 1 dc into next 3 sts, 5 ch; rep from * to end, 1 ss into 1st dc.

Cut yarn and secure end with a few stitches into chain stitch loop. Damp, pin out to size and leave to dry.

Saucer doily with star motif

Materials

1 x 50 g Tridalia crochet cotton no. 8 cotton (enough for 6 saucer doilies)
4 double-pointed 2,00 mm knitting needles
1,25 mm crochet hook

Size: 9 cm in diameter

Instructions

Cast on 6 sts (2 on each of 3 needles). Form a circle and knit 1 rnd.
1st rnd: * K1, yfd; rep from * to end.
2nd and every alt rnd: Knit.
3rd rnd: * K1, yfd, k1, yfd; rep from * to end.
5th rnd: * K2, yfd, k2, yfd; rep from * to end.
7th rnd: * K3, yfd, k3, yfd; rep from * to end.
9th rnd: * K4, yfd, k4, yfd; rep from * to end.
11th rnd: * K5, yfd, k5, yfd; rep from * to end.
13th rnd: * Sl 1, k1, psso, k7, k2 tog, yfd, k1, yfd; rep from * to end.
15th rnd: * Sl 1, k1, psso, k5, k2 tog, yfd, k1, yfd, sl 1, k1, psso, yfd; rep from * to end.
17th rnd: * Sl 1, k1, psso, k3, k2 tog, yfd, k1, (yfd, sl 1, k1, psso) twice, yfd; rep from * to end.
19th rnd: * Sl 1, k1, psso, k1, k2 tog, yfd, k1, (yfd, sl 1, k1, psso) 3 times, yfd; rep from * to end.
20th rnd: Knit.

Crochet sts off as follows: * 1 dc into next 3 sts, 5 ch; rep from * to end, 1 ss in 1st dc.

Cut yarn and secure end with a few stitches into chain stitch loop. Damp, pin out to size and leave to dry.

Saucer doily with daisy motif

Materials

1 x 50 g Tridalia crochet cotton no. 8 (enough for 6 saucer doilies)
4 double-pointed 2,00 mm knitting needles
1,25 mm crochet hook

Size: 9 cm in diameter

Abbreviations: m9 – make 9 stitches = k1, (p1, k1) 4 times into the double loop of "yrn twice" of previous rnd (= 9 sts)

Instructions

Cast on 10 sts and divide onto 3 needles (2, 4, 4). Form circle and knit 1 rnd. Rnds not mentioned: knit.
1st rnd: * K1, yrn twice, k1; rep from * to end.

2nd rnd: * K1, m9 in "yrn twice" of previous rnd, k1; rep from * to end.

3rd to 6th rnd: * K11; rep from * to end.

7th rnd: * Yfd, k11; rep from * to end.

9th rnd: * Yfd, k1, yfd, k11; rep from * to end.

11th rnd: * Yfd, k3, yfd, sl 1, k1, psso, k7, k2 tog; rep from * to end.

13th rnd: * Yfd, k1, yfd, sl 1, k2 tog, psso, yfd, k1, yfd, sl 1, k1, psso, k5, k2 tog; rep from * to end.

15th rnd: * Yfd, k3, yfd, k1 tbl, yfd, k3, yfd, sl 1, k1, psso, k3, k2 tog; rep from * to end.

17th rnd: * Yfd, k1, yfd, (sl 1, k2 tog, psso, yfd) 3 times, k1, yfd, sl 1, k1, psso, k1, k2 tog; rep from * to end.

19th rnd: * Yfd, k3, (yfd, k1 tbl, yfd, k3) twice, yfd, sl 1, k2 tog, psso; rep from * to end.

20th rnd: Knit.

Knit 1 st and crochet sts off as follows: * 1 dc into next 3 sts, 4 ch: rep from * to end, 1 ss in 1st dc.

Cut yarn and secure end with a few stitches into chain stitch loop. Damp, pin out to size and leave to dry.

Knitted lace border for oval mirror frame

Materials

1 × 50 g Tridalia crochet cotton no. 8
4 double-pointed 2,50 mm knitting needles: 30 cm long, or
2,50 circular knitting needle: 60 cm long
1,50 mm crochet hook

Width of knitted border: 10 cm
Circumference of mirror: 91 cm

Abbreviations: m2 – make 2 stitches = k1, p1 and k1 into next st

Instructions

Cast on 204 sts (68 sts on each of 3 needles or 204 sts on circular needle) and knit 3 rnds.
4th rnd: * Sl 1, k2 tog, psso, yfd, k2 tog, yfd, k10, yfd, sl 1, k1, psso, yfd; rep from * to end.
5th rnd: Knit.
6th rnd: * K1, k2 tog, yfd, k4, k2 tog, yrn twice, sl 1, k1, psso, k4, yfd, sl 1, k1, psso; rep from * to end.
7th and every alt rnd: Knit, but k1, p1 into each "yrn twice" of previous rnd.
8th rnd: Transfer 2 sts from left to right and mark new beg of rnd. When sts are transferred at the beg of a rnd, remember to adjust sts on other needles as well.
The number of sts in each rnd is given in brackets at the end of each rnd, except where the number of sts in consecutive rnds remains the same.
* Yfd, k4, k2 tog (m2) twice, sl 1, k1, psso, k4, yfd, sl 1, k2 tog, psso; rep from * to end (= 228 sts).
10th rnd: * K4, k2 tog, k1 tbl, p1, k1 tbl, yrn twice, k1 tbl, p1, k1 tbl, sl 1, k1, psso, k3, k2 tog, yfd; rep from * to end.
11th and every alt rnd: As 7th rnd, but knit tbl all sts worked tbl in previous rnd and p each p st from previous rnd.
12th rnd: * K3, k2 tog, k1 tbl, p1, k1 tbl, (m2) twice, k1 tbl, p1, k1 tbl, sl 1, k1, psso, k4; rep from * to end (= 252 sts).

14th rnd: * K2, k2 tog, (k1 tbl, p1, k1 tbl) twice, yrn twice, (k1 tbl, p1, k1 tbl) twice, sl 1, k1, psso, k3; rep from * to end.
16th rnd: * K1, k2 tog, (k1 tbl, p1, k1 tbl) twice, (m2) twice, (k1 tbl, p1, k1 tbl) twice, sl 1, k1, psso, k2; rep from * to end (= 276 sts).
18th rnd: * K2 tog, (k1 tbl, p1, k1 tbl) 3 times, yrn twice, (k1 tbl, p1, k1 tbl) 3 times, sl 1, k1, psso, k1; rep from * to end.
20th rnd: Transfer 1 st from left to right, * (k1 tbl, p1, k1 tbl) 3 times, (m2) twice, (k1 tbl, p1, k1 tbl) 3 times, sl 1, k2 tog, psso; rep from * to end (= 300 sts).
22nd rnd: * (K1 tbl, p1, k1 tbl) 4 times, yfd, (k1 tbl, p1, k1 tbl) 4 times, yfd, k1 tbl, yfd; rep from * to end (= 336 sts).
24th rnd: * (K1 tbl, p1, k1 tbl) 4 times, m2, (k1 tbl, p1, k1 tbl) 4 times, yfd, sl 1, k2 tog, psso, yfd; rep from * to end.
26th, 28th and 30th rnds: * (K1 tbl, p1, k1 tbl) 9 times, yfd, sl 1, k2 tog, psso, yfd; rep from * to end.
32nd rnd: Knit, but knit tbl all sts worked tbl in previous rnd and p each p st from previous rnd (= 360 sts).

Crochet sts off as follows: * 1 dc into next 3 sts, 10 ch; rep from * to end, 1 ss into 1st dc.

Cut yarn and secure yarn end with a few sts into chain stitch loop. Finish off the inner edge by crocheting 1 row of dc around it, followed by a picot edge.

Damp, pin out in an oval and leave to dry. If preferred the lace border can be adapted for a round mirror simply by pinning it out in a circle instead of an oval.

The frame of the mirror in the photograph was made of hardboard which was first padded with a thick layer of wadding and then covered with calico. The mirror was glued into position in the centre and the knitted border sewn around the outer edge.

The lace border can be turned into a centrepiece by sewing it around the outer edge of a round or oval-shaped piece of fine cotton fabric.

Round tablecloth

Materials

6 × 50 g Tridalia crochet cotton no. 5
5 double-pointed 2,50 mm knitting needles: 30 cm long
2,50 mm circular knitting needle: 80 cm long
2,50 mm circular knitting needle: 100 cm long
2,00 mm steel crochet hook

Size: 115 cm in diameter

Abbreviations: m1 – make 1 stitch = knit into front and back of next st

Instructions

Cast on 8 sts (2 on each of 4 needles). Form a circle and knit 1st rnd.
2nd rnd: Knit.
3rd rnd: * Yrn twice, k1; rep from * to end (= 24 sts).
4th and every alt rnd unless otherwise stated: Knit, but k1, p1 into each "yrn twice" of previous rnd.
5th rnd: As 3rd rnd (= 72 sts).
The number of stitches in each pattern repeat, the number of repeats in every rnd and the total number of sts in each rnd are given in brackets at the end of each rnd.
7th rnd: * Yfd, k6; rep from * to end (7 × 12 = 84 sts).
9th rnd: * Yfd, k1, yfd, sl 1, k1, psso, k2, k2 tog; rep from * to end (7 × 12 = 84 sts).
11th rnd: * Yfd, k3, yfd, k4 tog; rep from * to end (6 × 12 = 72 sts).
13th rnd: * Yfd, k5, yfd, k1; rep from * to end (8 × 12 = 96 sts).
15th rnd: Transfer 1 st from left to right and mark new beg of rnd. When sts are transferred at the beg of a rnd, remember to adjust sts on other needles as well. * Yfd, sl 1, k1, psso, k1, k2 tog, yfd, k3; rep from * to end (8 × 12 = 96 sts).
17th rnd: Transfer 1 st from left to right, * yfd, sl 1, k2 tog, psso, yfd, k5; rep from * to end (8 × 12 = 96 sts).
19th rnd: Transfer 1 st from left to right, * yrn twice, k1, yrn twice, sl 1, k1, psso, k3, k2 tog; rep from * to end (10 × 12 = 120 sts).
21st rnd: Transfer 1 st from left to right, * yrn twice, sl 1, k2 tog, psso, yrn twice, sl 1, k1, psso, k3, k2 tog; rep from * to end (10 × 12 = 120 sts).
23rd and 25th rnds: Transfer 1 st from left to right. Work as 21st rnd from *.
27th rnd: Transfer 1 st from left to right, * yfd, k3, yfd, sl 1, k1, psso, k3, k2 tog; rep from * to end (10 × 12 = 120 sts).
29th rnd: * Yfd, k1, yfd, sl 1, k2 tog, psso, yfd, k1, yfd, sl 1, k1, psso, k1, k2 tog; rep from * to end (10 × 12 = 120 sts).
31st rnd: * Yfd, k3, m1, k3, yfd, sl 1, k2 tog, psso; rep from * to end (11 × 12 = 132 sts).
33rd rnd: * K3, sl 1, k1, psso, yrn twice, sl 1, k1, psso, k3, m1; rep from * to end (12 × 12 = 144 sts).
35th rnd: Transfer 1 st from left to right, * sl 1, k1, psso, yrn twice, sl 1, k1, psso; rep from * to end (4 × 36 = 144 sts).
37th rnd: * Yrn twice, (sl 1, k1, psso) twice; rep from * to end (4 × 36 = 144 sts).
39th rnd: Transfer 1 st from left to right, * sl 1, k1, psso, yrn twice, sl 1, k1, psso; rep from * to end (4 × 36 = 144 sts).
41st rnd: As 37th rnd.
43rd rnd: Transfer 1 st from left to right, * yrn twice, (sl 1, k1, psso) twice, yrn twice, (sl 1, k1, psso) twice, yrn twice, sl 1, k1, psso, k2 tog; rep from * to end (12 × 12 = 144 sts).
45th rnd: * Yrn twice, p2, yrn twice, sl 1, k1, psso, k1, sl 1, k1, psso, yrn twice, sl 1, k1, psso, k2 tog; rep from * to end (14 × 12 = 168 sts).
Purl each p st from previous rnd in rnds with even numbers.
47th rnd: * Yrn twice, k2 tbl, p2, k2 tbl, yrn twice, sl 1, k1, psso, k4, k2 tog; rep from * to end (16 × 12 = 192 sts). In rnds with even numbers, knit tbl all sts worked tbl in previous rnd.
49th rnd: Yrn twice, p2, k2 tbl, p2, k2 tbl, p2, yrn twice, sl 1, k1, psso, k2, k2 tog; rep from * to end (18 × 12 = 216 sts).
51st rnd: * Yrn twice, (k2 tbl, p2) 3 times, k2 tbl, yrn twice, k4 tog; rep from * to end (19 × 12 = 228 sts).
52nd rnd: * P1, k1 into "yrn twice" of previous rnd, (k2 tbl, p2) 3 times, k2 tbl, p1, k1 into "yrn twice" of previous rnd, m1; rep from * to end (20 × 12 = 240 sts).
53rd rnd: * (P2, k2 tbl) 5 times; rep from * to end (20 × 12 = 240 sts).
55th, 57th and 59th rnds: As 53rd rnd.
61st rnd: Transfer 1 st from right to left, * yfd, k1 tbl, (p2, k2 tbl) 4 times, p2, k1 tbl; rep from * to end (21 × 12 = 252 sts).
Change to 80 cm circular needle.
63rd rnd: * Yfd, k1, yfd, k1 tbl, (p2, k2 tbl) 4 times, p2, k1 tbl; rep from * to end (23 × 12 = 276 sts).
65th rnd: * Yfd, k3, yfd, k1 tbl, (p2, k2 tbl) 4 times, p2, k1 tbl; rep from * to end (25 × 12 = 300 sts).
67th rnd: * Yfd, k5, yfd, k4 tog, yfd, k1 tbl, (p2, k2 tbl) twice, p2, k1 tbl, yfd, k4 tog; rep from * to end (23 × 12 = 276 sts).
69th rnd: * Yfd, k7, yfd, sl 1, k1, psso, yfd, k1 tbl, (p2, k2 tbl) twice, p2, k1 tbl, yfd, k2 tog; rep from * to end (25 × 12 = 300 sts).
71st rnd: * Yfd, k9, yfd, sl 1, k1, psso, yfd, k4 tog, yfd, k1 tbl, p2, k1 tbl, yfd, k4 tog, yfd, k2 tog; rep from * to end (23 ×

12 = 276 sts).

73rd rnd: * Yfd, k1, yfd, k9, yfd, k1, yfd, (sl 1, k1, psso, yfd) twice, k1 tbl, p2, k1 tbl, (yfd, k2 tog) twice; rep from * to end (27 × 12 = 324 sts).

75th rnd: * Yfd, k2 tog, yfd, k1, yfd, sl 1, k1, psso, k5, k2 tog, yfd, k1, (yfd, sl 1, k1, psso) 3 times, yfd, k4 tog, (yfd, k2 tog) twice; rep from * to end (26 × 12 = 312 sts).

77th rnd: * (Yfd, k2 tog) twice, yfd, k1, yfd, k7, yfd, k1, (yfd, sl 1, k1, psso) 4 times, yfd, k1, (yfd, k2 tog) twice; rep from * to end (30 × 12 = 360 sts).

79th rnd: * (Yfd, k2 tog) 3 times, yfd, k1, yfd, sl 1, k1, psso, k3, k2 tog, yfd, k1, (yfd, sl 1, k1, psso) 5 times, k1, k2 tog, yfd, k2 tog; rep from * to end (30 × 12 = 360 sts).

81st rnd: * (Yfd, k2 tog) 4 times, yfd, k1, yfd, sl 1, k1, psso, k1, k2 tog, yfd, k1, (yfd, sl 1, k1, psso) 5 times, yfd, sl 1, k2 tog, psso, yfd, k2 tog; rep from * to end (30 × 12 = 360 sts).

82nd rnd: * K11, sl 1, k2 tog, psso, k16; rep from * to end (28 × 12 = 336 sts).

83rd rnd: * (Yfd, k2 tog) 5 times, yfd, k3, (yfd, sl 1, k1, psso) 6 times, k1, k2 tog; rep from * to end (28 × 12 = 336 sts).

85th rnd: * (Yfd, k2 tog) 6 times, yfd, k1, (yfd, sl 1, k1, psso) 6 times, yfd, sl 1, k2 tog, psso; rep from * to end (28 × 12 = 336 sts).

87th rnd: * (K2 tog, yfd) 6 times, k3, (yfd, sl 1, k1, psso) 6 times, k1; rep from * to end (28 × 12 = 336 sts).

89th rnd: Transfer 1 st from left to right, * (yfd, k2 tog) 6 times, yfd, k1, yfd, (sl 1, k1, psso, yfd) 6 times, sl 1, k2 tog, psso; rep from * to end (28 × 12 = 336 sts).

91st rnd: * (K2 tog, yfd) 6 times, k3, (yfd, sl 1, k1, psso) 6 times, k1; rep from * to end (28 × 12 = 336 sts).

93rd rnd: Transfer 1 st from left to right, * (yfd, k2 tog) 6 times, yfd, k1, yfd, (sl 1, k1, psso, yfd) 6 times, sl 1, k2 tog, psso; rep from * to end (28 × 12 = 336 sts).

95th rnd: * (K2 tog, yfd) 6 times, k3, (yfd, sl 1, k1, psso) 6 times, k1; rep from * to end (28 × 12 = 336 sts).

97th rnd: Transfer 1 st from left to right, * (yfd, k2 tog) 5 times, yfd, k2, yfd, k1, yfd, k2, yfd, (sl 1, k1, psso, yfd) 5 times, sl 1, k2 tog, psso; rep from * to end (30 × 12 = 360 sts).

99th rnd: * (K2 tog, yfd) 5 times, k3, yfd, sl 1, k2 tog, psso, yfd, k3, (yfd, sl 1, k1, psso) 5 times, k1; rep from * to end (30 × 12 = 360 sts).

101st rnd: Transfer 1 st from left to right, * (yfd, k2 tog) 4 times, yfd, k4, yfd, sl 1, k2 tog, psso, yfd, k4, yfd, (sl 1, k1, psso, yfd) 4 times, sl 1, k2 tog, psso; rep from * to end (30 × 12 = 360 sts).

103rd rnd: * (K2 tog, yfd) 4 times, k2, yfd, k1, yfd, k2, yfd, sl 1, k2 tog, psso, yfd, k2, yfd, k1, yfd, k2, (yfd, sl 1, k1, psso) 4 times, k1; rep from * to end (34 × 12 = 408 sts).

105th rnd: Transfer 1 st from left to right, * (yfd, k2 tog) 3 times, yfd, sl 1, k1, psso, k1, (yrn twice, sl 1, k2 tog, psso, yrn twice, k2) twice, yrn twice, sl 1, k2 tog, psso, yrn twice, k1, k2 tog, (yfd, sl 1, k1, psso) 3 times, yfd, sl 1, k2 tog, psso; rep from * to end (38 × 12 = 456 sts).

107th rnd: * (K2 tog, yfd) 3 times, sl 1, k1, psso, k2, (yrn twice, sl 1, k2 tog, psso, yrn twice, k4) twice, yrn twice, sl 1, k2 tog, psso, yrn twice, k2, k2 tog, (yfd, sl 1, k1, psso) 3 times, k1; rep from * to end (42 × 12 = 504 sts).

109th rnd: Transfer 1 st from left to right, * (yfd, k2 tog) twice, yfd, sl 1, k1, psso, k3, (yrn twice, sl 1, k2 tog, psso, yrn twice, k6) twice, yrn twice, sl 1, k2 tog, psso, yrn twice, k3, k2 tog, yfd, (sl 1, k1, psso, yfd) twice, sl 1, k2 tog, psso; rep from * to end (46 × 12 = 552 sts).

111th rnd: * (K2 tog, yfd) twice, sl 1, k1, psso, k4, (yrn twice, sl 1, k2 tog, psso, yrn twice, k8) twice, yrn twice, sl 1, k2 tog, psso, yrn twice, k4, k2 tog, (yfd, sl 1, k1, psso) twice, k1; rep from * to end (50 × 12 = 600 sts).

113th rnd: Transfer 1 st from left to right, * yfd, k2 tog, yfd, sl 1, k1, psso, k5, (yrn twice, sl 1, k2 tog, psso, yrn twice, k10) twice, yrn twice, sl 1, k2 tog, psso, yrn twice, k5, k2 tog, yfd, sl 1, k1, psso, yfd, sl 1, k2 tog, psso; rep from * to end (54 × 12 = 648 sts).

Change to 100 cm circular needle.

115th rnd: * K2 tog, yfd, sl 1, k1, psso, k6, (yrn twice, sl 1, k2 tog, psso, yrn twice, k12) twice, yrn twice, sl 1, k2 tog, psso, yrn twice, k6, k2 tog, yfd, sl 1, k1, psso, k1; rep from * to end (58 × 12 = 696 sts).

117th rnd: Transfer 1 st from left to right, * sl 1, k1, psso, k18, yfd, k6, yrn twice, sl 1, k2 tog, psso, yrn twice, k6, yfd, k18, k2 tog, yfd, sl 1, k2 tog, psso, yfd; rep from * to end (60 × 12 = 720 sts).

119th rnd: * Sl 1, k1, psso, k15, k2 tog, yfd, k8, yrn twice, sl 1, k2 tog, psso, yrn twice, k8, yfd, sl 1, k1, psso, k15, k2 tog, yfd, sl 1, k2 tog, psso, yfd; rep from * to end (60 × 12 = 720 sts).

121st rnd: * Sl 1, k1, psso, k13, k2 tog, yfd, sl 1, k1, psso, k8, yrn twice, sl 1, k2 tog, psso, yrn twice, k8, k2 tog, yfd, sl 1, k1, psso, k13, k2 tog, yfd, sl 1, k2 tog, psso, yfd; rep from * to end (58 × 12 = 696 sts).

123rd rnd: * Sl 1, k1, psso, k11, k2 tog, yfd, sl 1, k1, psso, k9, yrn twice, sl 1, k2 tog, psso, yrn twice, k9, k2 tog, yfd, sl 1, k1, psso, k11, k2 tog, yfd, sl 1, k2 tog, psso, yfd; rep from * to end (56 × 12 = 672 sts).

125th rnd: * Sl 1, k1, psso, k4, yfd, k1, yfd, k4, k2 tog, yfd, sl 1, k1, psso, k23, k2 tog, yfd, sl 1, k1, psso, k4, yfd, k1, yfd, k4, k2 tog, yfd, sl 1, k2 tog, psso, yfd; rep from * to end (56 × 12 = 672 sts).

127th rnd: * Sl 1, k1, psso, k3, sl 1, k2 tog, psso, k3, k2 tog, yfd, k1, yfd, sl 1, k1, psso, k21, k2 tog, yfd, k1, yfd, sl 1, k1, psso, k3, sl 1, k2 tog, psso, k3, k2 tog, yfd, sl 1, k2 tog, psso, yfd; rep from * to end (50 × 12 = 600 sts).

129th rnd: * Sl 1, k1, psso, k5, k2 tog, yfd, sl 1, k2 tog, psso, yfd, sl 1, k1, psso, k19, k2 tog, yfd, sl 1, k2 tog, psso, yfd, sl 1, k1, psso, k5, k2 tog, yfd, sl 1, k2 tog, psso, yfd; rep from * to end (44 × 12 = 528 sts).

131st rnd: * Sl 1, k1, psso, k3, k2 tog, yfd, k1, m1, k1, yfd, sl 1, k1, psso, k17, k2 tog, yfd, k1, m1, k1, yfd, sl 1, k1, psso, k3, k2 tog, yfd, k1, m1, k1, yfd; rep from * to end (47 × 12 = 564 sts).

133rd rnd: * Sl 1, k1, psso, k1, k2 tog, yfd, k3, yrn twice, k3, yfd, sl 1, k1, psso, k15, k2 tog, yfd, k3, yrn twice, k3, yfd, sl 1, k1, psso, k1, k2 tog, yfd, k3, yrn twice, k3, yfd; rep from * to end (53 × 12 = 636 sts).

134th rnd: * Sl 1, k2 tog, psso, k4, p1, k26, p1, k5, sl 1, k2 tog, psso, k4, p1, k5; rep from * to end (49 × 12 = 588 sts).

135th rnd: * M1, k3, yrn twice, (sl 1, k1, psso) twice, yrn twice, k3, yfd, sl 1, k1, psso, k13, k2 tog, yfd, k3, yrn twice, (sl 1, k1, psso) twice, yrn twice, k3, m1, k3, yrn twice, (sl 1, k1, psso) twice, yrn twice, k3; rep from * to end (57 × 12 = 684 sts).

137th rnd: * K4, (yrn twice, [sl 1, k1, psso] twice) twice, yrn twice, k3, yfd, sl 1, k1, psso, k5, yfd, k1, yfd, k5, k2 tog, yfd, k3, (yrn twice, [sl 1, k1, psso] twice) twice, yrn twice, k6, (yrn twice, [sl 1, k1, psso] twice) twice, yrn twice, k2; rep from * to end (65 × 12 = 780 sts).

139th rnd: Transfer 1 st from left to right, * sl 1, k1, psso, (yrn twice, [sl 1, k1, psso] twice) 3 times, yrn twice, k3, yfd, sl 1, k1, psso, k4, sl 1, k2 tog, psso, k4, k2 tog, yfd, k3, (yrn twice, [sl 1, k1, psso] twice) 7 times, yrn twice, sl 1, k1, psso; rep from * to end (65 × 12 = 780 sts).

141st rnd: * (Yrn twice, [sl 1, k1, psso] twice) 4 times, yrn twice, k3, yfd, sl 1, k1, psso, k7, k2 tog, yfd, k3, (yrn twice, [sl 1, k1, psso] twice) 8 times; rep from * to end (67 × 12 = 804 sts).

142nd rnd: * (P1, k3) 4 times, p1, k5, sl 1, k1, psso, k5, k2 tog, k4, (p1, k3) 8 times; rep from * to end (65 × 12 = 780 sts).

143rd rnd: Transfer 1 st from left to right, * sl 1, k1, psso, (yrn twice, [sl 1, k1, psso] twice) 4 times, yrn twice, k3, yfd, sl 1, k1, psso, k3, k2 tog, yfd, k3, (yrn twice, [sl 1, k1, psso] twice) 8 times, yrn twice, sl 1, k1, psso; rep from * to end (67 × 12 = 804 sts).

144th rnd: * K1, (p1, k3) 4 times, p1, k5, sl 1, k1, psso, k1, k2 tog, k4, (p1, k3) 8 times, p1, k2; rep from * to end (65 × 12 = 780 sts).

145th rnd: * (Yrn twice, [sl 1, k1, psso] twice) 5 times, yrn twice, k3, yfd, sl 1, k2 tog, psso, yfd, k3, (yrn twice, [sl 1, k1, psso] twice) 9 times; rep from * to end (67 × 12 = 804 sts).

146th rnd: * (P1, k3) 5 times, p1, k5, m1, k4, (p1, k3) 9 times; rep from * to end (68 × 12 = 816 sts).

147th rnd: Transfer 1 st from left to right, * (sl 1, k1, psso, yrn twice, sl 1, k1, psso) 6 times, k4, (sl 1, k1, psso, yrn twice, sl 1, k1, psso) 10 times; rep from * to end (68 × 12 = 816 sts).

149th rnd: * Yrn twice, (sl 1, k1, psso) twice; rep from * to end (4 × 204 = 816 sts).

151st rnd: Transfer 1 st from left to right, * sl 1, k1, psso, yrn twice, sl 1, k1, psso; rep from * to end (4 × 204 = 816 sts).

153rd rnd: Transfer 8 sts from left to right, * yfd, ([sl 1, k1, psso] twice, yrn twice) 8 times, sl 1, k1, psso, k2 tog, yfd, ([sl 1, k1, psso] twice, yrn twice) 7 times, sl 1, k1, psso, k2 tog; rep from * to end (66 × 12 = 792 sts).

155th rnd: * Yfd, k1, yfd, sl 1, k1, psso, k1, k2 tog, (yrn twice, [sl 1, k1, psso] twice) 6 times, yrn twice, sl 1, k1, psso, k1, k2 tog, yfd, k1, yfd, sl 1, k1, psso, k1, k2 tog, (yrn twice, [sl 1, k1, psso] twice) 5 times, yrn twice, sl 1, k1, psso, k1, k2 tog; rep from * to end (66 × 12 = 792 sts).

157th rnd: * Yfd, k3, yfd, sl 1, k1, psso, k2, k2 tog, (yrn twice, [sl 1, k1, psso] twice) 5 times, yrn twice, sl 1, k1, psso, k2, k2 tog, yfd, k3, yfd, sl 1, k1, psso, k2, k2 tog, (yrn twice, [sl 1, k1, psso] twice) 4 times, yrn twice, sl 1, k1, psso, k2, k2 tog; rep from * to end (66 × 12 = 792 sts).

159th rnd: * Yfd, k5, yfd, sl 1, k1, psso, k3, k2 tog, (yrn twice, [sl 1, k1, psso] twice) 4 times, yrn twice, sl 1, k1, psso, k3, k2 tog, yfd, k5, yfd, sl 1, k1, psso, k3, k2 tog, (yrn twice, [sl 1, k1, psso] twice) 3 times, yrn twice, sl 1, k1, psso, k3, k2 tog; rep from * to end (66 × 12 = 792 sts).

160th rnd: * K7, sl 1, k1, psso, (k3, p1) 5 times, k4, k2 tog, k7, sl 1, k1, psso, (k3, p1) 4 times, k4, k2 tog; rep from * to end (62 × 12 = 744 sts).

161st rnd: * Yfd, k7, yfd, sl 1, k1, psso, k3, (sl 1, k1, psso, yrn twice, sl 1, k1, psso) 4 times, k3, k2 tog, yfd, k7, yfd, sl 1, k1, psso, k3, (sl 1, k1, psso, yrn twice, sl 1, k1, psso) 3 times, k3, k2 tog; rep from * to end (62 × 12 = 744 sts).

163rd rnd: * Yfd, k4, m1, k4, yfd, sl 1, k1, psso, k4, (sl 1, k1, psso, yrn twice, sl 1, k1, psso) 3 times, k4, k2 tog, yfd, k4, m1, k4, yfd, sl 1, k1, psso, k4, (sl 1, k1, psso, yrn twice, sl 1, k1, psso) twice, k4, k2 tog; rep from * to end (64 × 12 = 768 sts).

165th rnd: * Yfd, k3, sl 1, k2 tog, psso, yrn 3 times, sl 1, k2 tog, psso, k3, yfd, sl 1, k1, psso, k5, (sl 1, k1, psso, yrn twice, sl 1, k1, psso) twice, k5, k2 tog, yfd, k3, sl 1, k2 tog, psso, yrn 3 times, sl 1, k2 tog, psso, k3, yfd, sl 1, k1, psso, k5, sl 1, k1, psso, yrn twice, sl 1, k1, psso, k5, k2 tog; rep from * to end (62 × 12 = 744 sts).

166th rnd: Knit, but (k1, p1) 4 times into each "yrn 3 times" of previous rnd (72 × 12 = 864 sts).

167th rnd: * Yfd, k18, yfd, sl 1, k1, psso, k6, sl 1, k1, psso, yrn twice, sl 1, k1, psso, k6, k2 tog, yfd, k18, yfd, k16; rep from * to end (74 × 12 = 888 sts).

169th rnd: * Yfd, k20, yfd, sl 1, k1, psso, k5, (sl 1, k1, psso) twice, k5, k2 tog, yfd, k20, yfd, sl 1, k1, psso, k12, k2 tog; rep from * to end (72 × 12 = 864 sts).

171st rnd: * Yfd, sl 1, k1, psso, k4, yfd, k5, yfd, k5, yfd, k4, k2 tog, yfd, sl 1, k1, psso, k10, k2 tog; rep from * to end (37 × 24 = 888 sts).

173rd rnd: * (Yfd, k1, yfd, sl 1, k1, psso, k1, k2 tog) 4 times, yfd, k1, yfd, sl 1, k1, psso, k8, k2 tog; rep from * to end (37 × 24 = 888 sts).

175th rnd: * Yfd, (k3, yfd, sl 1, k2 tog, psso, yfd) 4 times, k3, yfd, sl 1, k1, psso, k6, k2 tog; rep from * to end (37 × 24 = 888 sts).

177th rnd: * Yfd, (k5, yfd, k1, yfd) 4 times, k5, yfd, sl 1, k1, psso, k4, k2 tog; rep from * to end (45 × 24 = 1080 sts).

178th rnd: Knit.

Crochet sts off as follows: 1 dc into next 6 sts, 9 ch, (1 dc into next 3 sts, 9 ch, 1 dc into next 5 sts, 9 ch) 3 times, 1 dc into next 3 sts, 9 ch, (1 dc into next 6 sts, 5 ch) twice; rep from * to end, 1 ss into 1st dc.

Cut yarn and work in yarn end. Damp, pin out to size and leave to dry.

Decorations for cushion covers

Round cushion front

Materials

1 × 50 g Tridalia crochet cotton no. 8
5 double-pointed 2,50 mm knitting needles: 30 cm long
1,50 mm crochet hook

Size: 33 cm in diameter

Instructions

Cast on 10 sts and divide onto 4 needles (2, 2, 3, 3). Form a circle and knit 2 rnds.
3rd rnd: (Yfd, k1) 10 times.
4th and 5th rnds: Knit.
6th rnd: (Yrn twice, k2 tog) 10 times.
7th rnd: (K1, p1, k1) 10 times.
8th rnd: Transfer 1 st from left to right and mark new beg of rnd. When sts are transferred at the beg of a rnd, remember to adjust sts on other needles as well. Knit to end.
9th rnd: (Yrn twice, k3) 10 times.
10th rnd: (K1, p1, k3) 10 times.
11th rnd: Transfer 1 st from left to right, knit to end.
12th rnd: (Yrn twice, k1, p3 tog, k1) 10 times.
13th rnd: (K1, p1, k3) 10 times.
14th rnd: Transfer 1 st from left to right, knit to end.
15th rnd: (Yrn twice, k5) 10 times.
16th rnd: (K1, p1, k5) 10 times.
17th rnd: Transfer 1 st from left to right, knit to end.
18th rnd: (Yrn twice, k2, p3 tog, k2) 10 times.
19th rnd: (K1, p1, k5) 10 times.
20th rnd: Transfer 1 st from left to right, knit to end.
21st rnd: (Yrn twice, k7) 10 times.
22nd rnd: (K1, p1, k7) 10 times.
23rd rnd: Transfer 1 st from left to right, knit to end.
24th rnd: (Yrn twice, k3, p3 tog, k3) 10 times.
25th rnd: (K1, p1, k7) 10 times.
26th rnd: Transfer 1 st from left to right, knit to end.
27th rnd: (Yrn twice, k9) 10 times.
28th rnd: (K1, p1, k9) 10 times.
29th rnd: Transfer 1 st from left to right, knit to end.
30th rnd: (Yfd, k4, p3 tog, k4) 10 times.
31st and every alt rnd unless otherwise stated: Knit.
32nd rnd: (Yfd, k1, yfd, k9) 10 times.
34th rnd: (Yfd, k3, yfd, k3, p3 tog, k3) 10 times.
36th rnd: (Yfd, k2 tog, yfd, k1, yfd, sl 1, k1, psso, yfd, k7) 10 times.

38th rnd: (Yfd, k2 tog, yfd, k3, yfd, sl 1, k1, psso, yfd, k2, p3 tog, k2) 10 times.
40th rnd: ([Yfd, k2 tog] twice, yfd, k1, [yfd, sl 1, k1, psso] twice, yfd, k5) 10 times.
42nd rnd: ([Yfd, k2 tog] twice, yfd, k3, [yfd, sl 1, k1, psso] twice, yfd, k1, p3 tog, k1) 10 times.
44th rnd: ([Yfd, k2 tog] 3 times, yfd, k1, [yfd, sl 1, k1, psso] 3 times, yfd, k3) 10 times.
46th rnd: ([Yfd, k2 tog] 3 times, yfd, k3, [yfd, sl 1, k1, psso] 3 times, yfd, p3 tog) 10 times.
48th rnd: ([K2 tog, yfd] 3 times, k5, [yfd, sl 1, k1, psso] 3 times, k1) 10 times.
50th rnd: K1, ([yfd, k2 tog] twice, yfd, k3, yrn twice, sl 1, k1, psso, k2, [yfd, sl 1, k1, psso] twice, yfd, sl 1, k2 tog, psso) 10 times. Work last dec at end of rnd with 1st st on 1st needle. Beg of rnd therefore moves 1 st to the left.
51st rnd: (K9, p1, k9) 10 times.
52nd rnd: ([K2 tog, yfd] twice, k10, [yfd, sl 1, k1, psso] twice, k1) 10 times.
53rd rnd: (K7, yrn twice, k2 tog, yrn twice, sl 1, k1, psso, yrn twice, k8) 10 times.
54th rnd: K1, (yfd, k2 tog, yfd, k5, p1, k2, p1, k2, p1, k4, yfd, sl 1, k1, psso, yfd, sl 1, k2 tog, psso) 10 times. Work last dec at end of rnd with 1st st on 1st needle.
55th rnd: Knit.
56th rnd: (K2 tog, yfd, k6, yrn twice, [k3, yrn twice] twice, k6, yfd, sl 1, k1, psso, k1) 10 times.
57th rnd: (K9, p1, k4, p1, k4, p1, k9) 10 times.
58th rnd: K1, (yfd, k26, yfd, sl 1, k2 tog, psso) 10 times. Work last dec at end of rnd with 1st st on 1st needle.
59th rnd: (K9, yrn twice, [k5, yrn twice] twice, k10) 10 times.
60th rnd: K1, (k2 tog, k7, [p1, k6] 3 times, sl 1, k1, psso, sl 1, k2 tog, psso) 10 times. Work last dec at end of rnd with 1st st on 1st needle.
61st rnd: K1, (k2 tog, k24, sl 1, k1, psso, sl 1, k2 tog, psso) 10 times. Work last dec at end of rnd with 1st st on 1st needle.

Slip last st of 61st rnd onto a crochet hook and crochet sts off as follows: * 1 dc into each of next 2 st, (1 dc into next 2 sts, 5 ch) 3 times, 1 dc into next 3 sts, (5 ch, 1 dc into next 2 sts) twice, 5 ch, 1 dc into next 3 sts, (5 ch, 1 dc into next 2 sts) 3 times, 1 dc into each of next 3 sts; rep from * 9 times.

Cut yarn and work in yarn end. Damp, pin out to size and leave to dry. Sew knitted front neatly onto cushion cover and finish off edge with a frill of gathered cotton lace or a knitted lace edging.

Square cushion front

Materials

1 × 50 g Tridalia crochet cotton no. 8
4 double-pointed 2,50 mm knitting needles: 30 cm long
1,50 mm crochet hook

Size: 30 cm × 30 cm

Instructions

Cast on 8 sts and divide onto 3 needles (2, 2, 4). Form a circle and knit 1 rnd. Mark beg of rnd.

1st rnd: Knit.
2nd rnd: * Yfd, k1; rep from * to end.
3rd and every alt rnd: Knit.
4th rnd: * Yfd, k3, yfd, k1 tbl; rep from * to end.
6th rnd: * Yfd, k5, yfd, k1 tbl; rep from * to end.
8th rnd: * Yfd, k7, yfd, k1 tbl; rep from * to end.
10th rnd: * Yfd, k3, k2 tog, yfd, k4, yfd, k1 tbl; rep from * to end.
12th rnd: * Yfd, k3, k2 tog, yfd, k1, yfd, sl 1, k1, psso, k3, yfd, k1 tbl; rep from * to end.
14th rnd: * Yfd, k3, k2 tog, yfd, k3 yfd, sl 1, k1, psso, k3, yfd, k1 tbl; rep from * to end.
16th rnd: * Yfd, k3, (k2 tog, yfd) twice, k1, (yfd, sl 1, k1, psso) twice, k3, yfd, k1 tbl; rep from * to end.
18th rnd: * Yfd, k3, (k2 tog, yfd) twice, k3, (yfd, sl 1, k1, psso) twice, k3, yfd, k1 tbl; rep from * to end.
20th rnd: As 16th rnd, but rep instructions in brackets ( ) 3 times.
22nd rnd: As 18th rnd, but rep instructions in brackets ( ) 3 times.
24th rnd: As 16th rnd, but rep instructions in brackets ( ) 4 times.
26th rnd: * K3, (k2 tog, yfd) 4 times, k3, (yfd, sl 1, k1, psso) 4 times, k3, yfd, k1 tbl, yfd; rep from * to end.
28th rnd: * Sl 1, k1, psso, k3, (yfd, sl 1, k1, psso) 3 times, (yfd, k1) 3 times, (yfd, k2 tog) 3 times, yfd, k3, k2 tog, yfd, k3, yfd; rep from * to end.
30th rnd: * Sl 1, k1, psso, k3, (yfd, sl 1, k1, psso) 3 times, yfd, k2 tog, yfd, k1, yfd, sl 1, k1, psso, (yfd, k2 tog) 3 times, yfd, k3, k2 tog, yfd, k5, yfd; rep from * to end.
32nd rnd: * Sl 1, k1, psso, k3, (yfd, sl 1, k1, psso) 3 times, yfd, k2 tog, yfd, k1 yfd, sl 1, k1, psso, (yfd, k2 tog) 3 times, yfd, k3, k2 tog, yfd, k7, yfd; rep from * to end.
34th rnd: * Sl 1, k1, psso, k3, (yfd, sl 1, k1, psso) 3 times, yfd, k2 tog, yfd, k1, yfd, sl 1, k1, psso, (yfd, k2 tog) 3 times, yfd, k3, k2 tog, yfd, k9, yfd; rep from * to end.
36th rnd: * Sl 1, k1, psso, k3, (yfd, sl 1, k1, psso) 4 times, k1, (k2 tog, yfd) 4 times, k3, k2 tog, yfd, sl 1, k1, psso, (yfd, k1 tbl) 7 times, yfd, k2 tog, yfd; rep from * to end.
38th rnd: * Sl 1, k1, psso, k3, (yfd, sl 1, k1, psso) 3 times, yfd, sl 1, k2 tog, psso, (yfd, k2 tog) 3 times, yfd, k3, k2 tog, yfd, sl 1, k1, psso, k1, (yfd, k1 tbl, yfd, k3) 3 times, yfd, k1 tbl, yfd, k1, k2 tog, yfd; rep from * to end.
40th rnd: * Sl 1, k1, psso, k3, (yfd, sl 1, k1, psso) 3 times, k1, (k2 tog, yfd) 3 times, k3, k2 tog, yfd, sl 1, k2 tog, psso, k1, (yfd, k1 tbl, yfd, k1, k2 tog, k2) 3 times, yfd, k1 tbl, yfd, k1, k3 tog, yfd; rep from * to end.
42nd rnd: * Sl 1, k1, psso, k3, (yfd, sl 1, k1, psso) twice, yfd, sl 1, k2 tog, psso, (yfd, k2 tog) twice, yfd, k3, k2 tog, yfd, sl 1, k1, psso, k2, (yfd, k1 tbl, yfd, k6) 3 times, yfd, k1 tbl, yfd, k2, k2 tog, yfd; rep from * to end.
44th rnd: * Sl 1, k1, psso, k3, (yfd, sl 1, k1, psso) twice, k1, (k2 tog, yfd) twice, k3, k2 tog, yfd, sl 1, k2 tog, psso, k2, (yfd, k1 tbl, yfd, k2, k2 tog, sl 1, k1, psso, k2) 3 times, yfd, k1 tbl, yfd, k2, k3 tog, yfd; rep from * to end.
46th rnd: * Sl 1, k1, psso, k3, yfd, sl 1, k1, psso, yfd, sl 1, k2 tog, psso, yfd, k2 tog, yfd, k3, k2 tog, yfd, sl 1, k1, psso, k3, (yfd, k1 tbl, yfd, k8) 3 times, yfd, k1 tbl, yfd, k3, k2 tog, yfd; rep from * to end.
48th rnd: * Sl 1, k1, psso, k3, yfd, sl 1, k1, psso, k1, k2 tog, yfd, k3, k2 tog, yfd, sl 1, k2 tog, psso, k3, (yfd, k1 tbl, yfd, k3, k2 tog, sl 1, k1, psso, k3) 3 times, yfd, k1 tbl, yfd, k3, k3 tog, yfd; rep from * to end.
50th rnd: * Sl 1, k1, psso, k3, yfd, sl 1, k2 tog, psso, yfd, k3, k2 tog, yfd, sl 1, k1, psso, k10, (yfd, k11) twice, yfd, k10, k2 tog, yfd; rep from * to end.
52nd rnd: * Sl 1, k1, psso, k7, k2 tog, yfd, k1 and p1 into next st, yfd; rep from * to end.
54th rnd: * Sl 1, k1, psso, k5, k2 tog, yfd, k4, yfd; rep from * to end.
56th rnd: * Sl 1, k1, psso, k3, k2 tog, yfd, k1, k2 tog, yrn twice, sl 1, k1, psso, k1, yfd; rep from * to end.
57th rnd: Knit, but k1, p1 and k1 into each "yrn twice" of previous rnd.
58th rnd: * Sl 1, k1, psso, k1, k2 tog, yfd, sl 1, k1, psso, k5, k2 tog, yfd; rep from * to end.
59th rnd: Knit.

Knit 1 st and then crochet sts off as follows: * 1 dc into next 3 sts, 12 ch; rep from * to end, 1 ss into 1st dc.

Cut yarn and work in yarn end. Damp, pin out to size and leave to dry.

Sew knitted front neatly onto cushion cover and finish off edge with a frill of gathered cotton lace or a knitted lace edging.

Square cheval set

Materials

1 × 50 g Tridalia crochet cotton no. 8
5 double-pointed 2,50 mm knitting needles: 30 cm long
1,25 mm crochet hook

Size: Centrepiece: 35 cm × 22 cm; small mats: 22 cm × 22 cm

Centrepiece

Instructions

Cast on 48 sts (16 sts on each of 3 needles). Form a circle and knit 1st rnd.
2nd rnd: * (Yfd, k1, yfd, sl 1, k2 tog, psso) 5 times, (yfd, k1, yfd, k1 tbl) twice; rep once from * to end.
3rd and every alt rnd: Knit.
4th rnd: * Yfd, k23, yfd, k1 tbl, yfd, k3, yfd, k1 tbl; rep once from * to end.
6th rnd: * (Yfd, k1, yfd, sl 1, k2 tog, psso) 6 times, yfd, k1, yfd, k1 tbl, yfd, k1, yfd, sl 1, k2 tog, psso, yfd, k1, yfd, k1 tbl; rep once from * to end.
Rearrange sts on 4 needles (28, 8, 28, 8).
8th rnd: * Yfd, k27, yfd, k1 tbl, yfd, k7, yfd, k1 tbl; rep once from * to end.
10th rnd: * (Yfd, k1, yfd, sl 1, k2 tog, psso) 7 times, yfd, k1, yfd, k1 tbl, (yfd, k1, yfd, sl 1, k2 tog, psso) twice, yfd, k1, yfd, k1 tbl; rep once from * to end.
12th rnd: * Yfd, k31, yfd, k1 tbl, yfd, k11, yfd, k1 tbl; rep once from * to end.
14th rnd: * (Yfd, k1, yfd, sl 1, k2 tog, psso) 8 times, yfd, k1, yfd, k1 tbl, (yfd, k1, yfd, sl 1, k2 tog, psso) 3 times, yfd, k1, yfd, k1 tbl; rep once from * to end.
16th rnd: * Yfd, k35, yfd, k1 tbl, yfd, k15, yfd, k1 tbl; rep once from * to end.
18th rnd: * (Yfd, k1, yfd, sl 1, k2 tog, psso) 9 times, yfd, k1, yfd, k1 tbl, (yfd, k1, yfd, sl 1, k2 tog, psso) 4 times, yfd, k1, yfd, k1 tbl; rep once from * to end.
20th rnd: * Yfd, k39, yfd, k1 tbl, yfd, k19, yfd, k1 tbl; rep once from * to end.
22nd rnd: * (Yfd, k1, yfd, sl 1, k2 tog, psso) 10 times, yfd, k1, yfd, k1 tbl, (yfd, k1, yfd, sl 1, k2 tog, psso) 5 times, yfd, k1, yfd, k1 tbl; rep once from * to end.
24th rnd: * (Yfd, k3, yfd, sl 1, k1, psso, k13, k2 tog) twice, yfd, k3, yfd, k1 tbl, yfd, k3, yfd, sl 1, k1, psso, k13, k2 tog, yfd, k3, yfd, k1 tbl; rep once from * to end.
26th rnd: * Yfd, k5, (yfd, sl 1, k2 tog, psso, yfd, k1) 3 times, yfd, sl 1, k2 tog, psso **; rep once from * to **, yfd, k5, yfd,

k1 tbl; rep once from * to **, yfd, k5, yfd, k1 tbl; rep once from * to end.
28th rnd: * Yfd, sl 1, k1, psso, k5, ** yfd, sl 1, k1, psso, k9, k2 tog, yfd **, k7; rep once from ** to **, k5, k2 tog, yfd, k1 tbl, yfd, sl 1, k1, psso, k5; rep once from ** to **, k5, k2 tog, yfd, k1 tbl; rep once from * to end.
30th rnd: * Yfd, sl 1, k2 tog, psso, k5, ** (yfd, sl 1, k2 tog, psso, yfd, k1) twice, yfd, sl 1, k2 tog, psso, yfd, k5 **, yfd, k4; rep once from ** to **, sl 1, k2 tog, psso, yfd, k1 tbl, yfd, sl 1, k2 tog, psso, k5; rep once from ** to **, sl 1, k2 tog, psso, yfd, k1 tbl; rep once from * to end.
32nd rnd: * Yfd, k1 tbl, (yfd, sl 1, k1, psso, k5) twice, k2 tog, yfd, k6, yfd, k1 tbl, yfd, k5, yfd, sl 1, k1, psso, (k5, k2 tog, yfd) twice, (k1 tbl, yfd) 3 times, sl 1, k1, psso, k5, yfd, sl 1, k1, psso, (k5, k2 tog, yfd) twice, k1 tbl, yfd, k1 tbl; rep once from * to end.
34th rnd: * Yfd, k3, yfd, sl 1, k1, psso, k5, yfd, sl 1, k2 tog, psso, yfd, k1, yfd, sl 1, k2 tog, psso, yfd, k5, k2 tog, yfd, k3, yfd **, k6, yfd, sl 1, k2 tog, psso, yfd, k1, yfd, sl 1, k2 tog, psso, yfd, k5, k2 tog, yfd, k3, yfd, k1 tbl; rep once from * to **, k1 tbl; rep once from * to end.
36th rnd: * Yfd, sl 1, k1, psso, yfd, k1 tbl, yfd, k2 tog, yfd, sl 1, k1, psso, k5, yfd, sl 1, k1, psso, k1, k2 tog, yfd, k5, k2 tog **; rep once from * to **, yfd, sl 1, k1, psso, yfd, k1 tbl, yfd, k2 tog, yfd, k1 tbl; rep once from * to **, yfd, sl 1, k1, psso, yfd, k1 tbl, yfd, k2 tog, yfd, k1 tbl; rep once from * to end.
38th rnd: * Yfd, sl 1, k1, psso, k1, yfd, k1 tbl, yfd, k1, k2 tog, yfd, sl 1, k1, psso, k5, yfd, sl 1, k2 tog, psso, yfd, k5, k2 tog **; rep once from * to **, yfd, sl 1, k1, psso, k1, yfd, k1 tbl, yfd, k1, k2 tog, yfd, k1 tbl; rep once from * to **, yfd, sl 1, k1, psso, k1, yfd, k1 tbl, yfd, k1, k2 tog, yfd, k1 tbl; rep once from * to end.
40th rnd: * Yfd, sl 1, k1, psso, k2, yfd, k1 tbl, yfd, k2, k2 tog, yfd, sl 1, k1, psso, k4, k2 tog, yfd, k5, k2 tog **; rep once from * to **, yfd, sl 1, k1, psso, k2, yfd, k1 tbl, yfd, k2, k2 tog, yfd, k1 tbl; rep once from * to **, yfd, sl 1, k1, psso, k2, yfd, k1 tbl, yfd, k2, k2 tog, yfd, k1 tbl; rep once from * to end.
42nd rnd: * Yfd, sl 1, k1, psso, k3, yfd, k1 tbl, yfd, k3, k2 tog, yfd, sl 1, k1, psso, k9, k2 tog **; rep once from * to **, yfd, sl 1, k1, psso, k3, yfd, k1 tbl, yfd, k3, k2 tog, yfd, k1 tbl; rep once from * to **, yfd, sl 1, k1, psso, k3, yfd, k1 tbl, yfd, k3, k2 tog, yfd, k1 tbl; rep once from * to end.
44th rnd: * Yfd, k1 tbl, yfd, sl 1, k1, psso, k7, k2 tog **; rep 4 times from * to **, (yfd, k1 tbl) twice; rep 3 times from * to **, (yfd, k1 tbl) twice; rep once from * to end.
46th rnd: * Yfd, k3, yfd, sl 1, k1, psso, k5, k2 tog **, rep 4 times from * to **, yfd, k3, yfd, k1 tbl; rep 3 times from * to **, yfd, k3, yfd, k1 tbl; rep once from * to end.
48th rnd: * Yfd, k1, yfd, sl 1, k2 tog, psso, yfd, k1, yfd, sl 1, k1, psso, k3, k2 tog **; rep 4 times from * to **, yfd, k1, yfd,

sl 1, k2 tog, psso, yfd, k1, yfd, k1 tbl; rep 3 times from * to **, yfd, k1, yfd, sl 1, k2 tog, psso, yfd, k1, yfd, k1 tbl; rep once from * to end.
50th rnd: * Yfd, k7, yfd, sl 1, k1, psso, k1, k2 tog **; rep 4 times from * to **, yfd, k7, yfd, k1 tbl; rep 3 times from * to **, yfd, k7, yfd, k1 tbl; rep once from * to end.
51st rnd: Knit.

Sl 1 st from left ro right and crochet sts off as follows: * 1 dc into next 2 sts, 10 ch, (1 dc into next 3 sts, 10 ch) 21 times, 1 dc into next 2 sts, 10 ch, 1 dc into next 3 sts, 10 ch, 1 dc into next 2 sts, 10 ch, (1 dc into next 3 sts, 10 ch) 13 times, 1 dc into next 2 sts, 10 ch, 1 dc into next 3 sts, 10 ch; rep once from * to end, 1 ss into 1st dc.

Cut yarn and work in yarn end.

Fold centrepiece in half lengthwise, with right sides facing, and neatly sew up the opening in the centre. Match pattern carefully. Cut yarn and work in yarn end. Damp, pin out to size and leave to dry.

Small mat (knit 2)

Instructions

Cast on 8 sts and divide onto 3 needles (2, 2, 4). Form a circle and knit 2 rnds.
3rd rnd: * Yfd, k1, yfd, k1 tbl; rep from * to end.
4th and every alt rnd: Knit.
5th rnd: * Yfd, k3, yfd, k1 tbl; rep from * to end.
7th rnd: * Yfd, k1, yfd, sl 1, k2 tog, psso, yfd, k1, yfd, k1 tbl; rep from * to end.
9th rnd: * Yfd, k7, yfd, k1 tbl; rep from * to end.
11th rnd: * (Yfd, k1, yfd, sl 1, k2 tog, psso) twice, yfd, k1, yfd, k1 tbl; rep from * to end.
13th rnd: * Yfd, k11, yfd, k1 tbl; rep from * to end.
15th rnd: * (Yfd, k1, yfd, sl 1, k2 tog, psso) 3 times, yfd, k1, yfd, k1 tbl; rep from * to end.
17th rnd: * Yfd, k15, yfd, k1 tbl; rep from * to end.
19th rnd: * (Yfd, k1, yfd, sl 1, k2 tog, psso) 4 times, yfd, k1, yfd, k1 tbl; rep from * to end.

21st rnd: * Yfd, k3, yfd, sl 1, k1, psso, k9, k2 tog, yfd, k3, yfd, k1 tbl; rep from * to end.
23rd rnd: * Yfd, k5, (yfd, sl 1, k2 tog, psso, yfd, k1) twice, yfd, sl1, k2 tog, psso, yfd, k5, yfd, k1 tbl; rep from * to end.
25th rnd: * Yfd, k1 tbl, yfd, sl 1, k1, psso, k4, yfd, sl 1, k1, psso, k5, k2 tog, yfd, k4, k2 tog, (yfd, k1 tbl) twice; rep from * to end.
27th rnd: * Yfd, k3, yfd, sl 1, k1, psso, k4, yfd, sl 1, k2 tog, psso, yfd, k1, yfd, sl 1, k2 tog, psso, yfd, k4, k2 tog, yfd, k3, yfd, k1 tbl; rep from * to end.
29th rnd: * Yfd, sl 1, k1, psso, yfd, k1 tbl, yfd, k2 tog, yfd, sl 1, k1, psso, k4, yfd, sl 1, k1, psso, k1, k2 tog, yfd, k4, k2 tog, yfd, sl 1, k1, psso, yfd, k1 tbl, yfd, k2 tog, yfd, k1 tbl; rep from * to end.
31st rnd: * Yfd, sl 1, k1, psso, k1, yfd, k1 tbl, yfd, k1, k2 tog, yfd, sl 1, k1, psso, k4, yfd, sl 1, k2 tog, psso, yfd, k4, k2 tog, yfd, sl 1, k1, psso, k1, yfd, k1 tbl, yfd, k1, k2 tog, yfd, k1 tbl; rep from * to end.
33rd rnd: * Yfd, sl 1, k1, psso, k2, yfd, k1 tbl, yfd, k1, k2 tog, yfd, sl 1, k1, psso, k3, k2 tog, yfd, k4, k2 tog, yfd, sl 1, k1, psso, k2, yfd, k1 tbl, yfd, k2, k2 tog, yfd, k1 tbl; rep from * to end.
35th rnd: * Yfd, k1 tbl, yfd, sl 1, k1, psso, k2, yfd, k1 tbl, yfd, k2, k2 tog, yfd, k1 tbl, yfd, sl 1, k1, psso, k7, k2 tog, yfd, k1 tbl, yfd, sl 1, k1, psso, k2, yfd, k1 tbl, yfd, k2, k2 tog, (yfd, k1 tbl) twice; rep from * to end.
37th rnd: * (Yfd, k3, yfd, sl 1, k1, psso, k5, k2 tog) 3 times, yfd, k3, yfd, k1 tbl; rep from * to end.
39th rnd: * (Yfd, k1, yfd, sl 1, k2 tog, psso, yfd, k1, yfd, sl 1, k1, psso, k3, k2 tog) 3 times, yfd, k1, yfd, sl 1, k2 tog, psso, yfd, k1, yfd, k1 tbl; rep from * to end.
41st rnd: * (Yfd, k7, yfd, sl 1, k1, psso, k1, k2 tog) 3 times, yfd, k7, yfd, k1 tbl; rep from * to end.
42nd rnd: Knit.

Sl 1 st from left to right and crochet sts off as follows: * 1 dc into next 2 sts, 8 ch, (1 dc into next 3 sts, 8 ch) 13 times, 1 dc into next 2 sts, 8 ch, 1 dc into next 3 sts, 8 ch; rep from * to end, 1 ss into 1st dc.

Cut yarn and work in yarn end. Damp, pin out to size and leave to dry.

Round cheval set

Materials

1 × 50 g Tridalia crochet cotton no. 8
4 double-pointed 2,50 mm knitting needles: 30 cm long
1,50 mm crochet hook

Size: Centrepiece: 30 cm in diameter; small mats: 22 cm in diameter

Centrepiece

Instructions

Cast on 8 sts and divide onto 3 needles (3, 3, 2). Form a circle and knit 2 rnds.
3rd rnd: * K1, p1 in next st, yrn twice; rep from * to end.
4th and every alt rnd: Knit, but k1, p1 into each "yrn twice" of previous rnd.
5th rnd: Transfer 1 st from left to right and mark new beg of rnd. When sts are transferred at beg of rnd, remember to adjust sts on other needles as well. * K2 tog tb1, yrn twice, k2 tog, yrn twice; rep from * to end.
7th rnd: * K2 tog tbl, yrn twice, k2 tog, k1, yrn twice, k1; rep from * to end.
9th rnd: * K2 tog tbl, yrn twice, k2 tog, k2, yrn twice, k2; rep from * to end.
11th rnd: * K2 tog tbl, yrn twice, k2 tog, k3, yrn twice, k3; rep from * to end.
13th rnd: * K2 tog tbl, yrn twice, k2 tog, k4, yrn twice, k4; rep from * to end.
15th rnd: * K9, yrn twice, k5; rep from * to end.
17th rnd: * K8, k2 tog, yrn twice, k2 tog tbl, k4; rep from * to end.
19th rnd: * K7, k2 tog, yfd, k2, yfd, k2 tog tbl, k3; rep from * to end.
21st rnd: * K6, k2 tog, yfd, k2 tog tbl, yrn twice, k2 tog, yfd, k2 tog tbl, k2; rep from * to end.
23rd rnd: * K5, k2 tog, yfd, k1, k2 tog tbl, yrn twice, k2 tog, k1, yfd, k2 tog tbl, k1; rep from * to end.
25th rnd: * K4, k2 tog, yfd, k2, k2 tog tbl, yrn twice, k2 tog, k2, yfd, k2 tog tbl; rep from * to end.
27th rnd: Transfer 2 sts from left to right, * k1, k2 tog, yfd, k3, k2 tog tbl, yrn twice, k2 tog, k3, yfd, k2 tog tbl, k1; rep from * to end.
29th rnd: * K2 tog, yfd, k4, k2 tog tbl, yrn twice, k2 tog, k4, yfd, k2 tog tbl; rep from * to end.
31st rnd: Transfer 1 st from left to right, * yrn twice, k5, k2 tog tbl, yrn twice, k2 tog, k5, yrn twice, sl 1, k1, psso; rep from * to end.

33rd rnd: * K1, yrn twice, k6, k2 tog tbl, yrn twice, k2 tog, k6, yrn twice, k2; rep from * to end.
35th rnd: * K2 tog tbl, yrn twice, k2 tog tbl, k14, k2 tog, yrn twice, k2 tog, yfd, k1, yfd; rep from * to end.
37th rnd: * Yfd, k2 tog tbl, yfd, k1, yrn twice, k2 tog tbl, k12, k2 tog, yrn twice, k1, yfd, k2 tog, yfd, k3; rep from * to end.
39th rnd: * K3, yfd, k2 tog tbl, yfd, k1, yrn twice, k2 tog tbl, k10, k2 tog, yrn twice, k1, yfd, k2 tog, yfd, k3, yfd, k3 tog, yfd; rep from * to end.
41st rnd: * Yfd, k3 tog, yfd, k1, (yfd, k2 tog tbl) twice, yfd, k1, yrn twice, k2 tog tbl, k8, k2 tog, yrn twice, k1, yfd, (k2 tog, yfd) twice, k1, yfd, k3 tog, yfd, k3; rep from * to end.
43rd rnd: * Yfd, k3 tog, yfd, k2 tog, yfd, (k3 tog, yfd) twice, k1, yrn twice, k2 tog tbl, k6, k2 tog, yrn twice, k1, yfd, (k3 tog, yfd) twice, k2 tog, (yfd, k3 tog) twice; rep from * to end.
45th rnd: * K2 tog, yfd, k3, yfd, k1, yfd, k3, yfd, k2 tog tbl, yfd, k1, yrn twice, k2 tog tbl, k4, k2 tog, yrn twice, k1, yfd, k2 tog, yfd, k3, yfd, k1, yfd, k3, yfd, k2 tog tbl, k1; rep from * to end.
47th rnd: Transfer 1 st from left to right, * (k2 tog tbl, k1, k2 tog, yfd, k1, yfd) twice, k3 tog, yfd, k1, yrn twice, k2 tog tbl, k2, k2 tog, yrn twice, k1, yfd, k3 tog, (yfd, k1, yfd, k2 tog tbl, k1, k2 tog) twice, yfd, sl 1, k2 tog, psso, yfd; rep from * to end.
49th rnd: * (Yfd, sl 1, k2 tog, psso, yfd, k3) twice, yfd, (k2 tog tbl) twice, yfd, k1, yfd, k2 tog tbl, k2 tog, yfd, k1, yfd, (k2 tog) twice, yfd (k3, yfd, sl 1, k2 tog, psso, yfd) twice, k3; rep from * to end.
50th rnd: Knit.

Crochet sts off as follows: * (1 dc into next 3 sts, 12 ch) twice, (1 dc into next 6 sts, 12 ch) twice, 1 dc into next 2 sts, (12 ch, 1 dc into next 6 sts,) twice, (12 ch, 1 dc into next 3 sts) 3 times, 12 ch; rep from * to end, 1 ss into 1st dc.

Cut yarn and work in yarn end. Damp, pin out to size and leave to dry.

Small mat (knit two)

Instructions

Work as centrepiece for 18 rnds.
19th rnd: * K7, (k2 tog, yrn 2 times) twice, k2 tog tbl, k3; rep from * to end.
21st rnd: * K6, k2 tog, yrn twice, k2 tog, yfd, k1, yfd, k2 tog, yrn twice, k2 tog tbl, k2; rep from * to end.
23rd rnd: * K5, k2 tog, yrn twice, k1, yfd, k2 tog, yfd, k3, yfd, k2 tog tbl, yfd, k1, yrn twice, k2 tog tbl, k1; rep from * to end.

25th rnd: * K4, k2 tog, yrn twice, k1, yfd, k2 tog, yfd, k3, yfd, k3 tog, yfd, k3, yfd, k2 tog tbl, yfd, k1, yrn twice, k2 tog tbl; rep from * to end.

27th rnd: Transfer 2 sts from left to right, * k1, k2 tog, yrn twice, k1, yfd, k2 tog, yfd, k3 tog, yfd, sl 1, k2 tog, psso, (yfd, k3 tog) 3 times, yfd, k2 tog tbl, yfd, k1, yrn twice, k2 tog, tbl, k1; rep from * to end.

29th rnd: * K2 tog, yfd, k1, yfd, k2 tog, yfd, k3, (yfd, k2 tog) twice, k1, k2 tog tbl, yfd, k2 tog, yfd, k3, yfd, k2 tog, yfd, k1, yfd, k2 tog tbl; rep from * to end.

30th rnd: Transfer 1 st from left to right. Knit.

Crochet sts off as follows: * (1 dc into next 4 sts, 12 ch) twice, (1 dc into next 3 sts, 12 ch) 3 times, (1 dc into next 4 sts, 12 ch) twice, 1 dc in next 2 sts, 12 ch; rep from * to end, 1 ss into 1st dc.

Cut yarn and work in yarn end. Damp, pin out to size and leave to dry.

Tray cloth and matching tea cosy

Materials

3 × 50 g Knit-Cro-Sheen crochet cotton no. 8
One pair 2,00 mm knitting needles: 30 cm long
1,50 mm crochet hook

Size: Tray cloth: 42 cm × 28 cm; tea cosy: 34 cm wide × 25 cm high; gusset for tea cosy: 4 cm × 72 cm

Abbreviations: mst – moss stitch = k1, p1 alternately.
Next row: k the p sts and p the k sts

Tray cloth

Instructions

Cast on 157 sts and work 14 rows in mst for border.
1st row: K1, (p1, k1) 6 times, * k24, (p1, k1) 6 times; rep from * to end.
2nd row: (K1, p1) 6 times, k1, * p23, (k1, p1) 6 times, k1; rep from * to end.
3rd row: As 1st row.
4th row: As 2nd row.
5th row: Mst 13, * k9, k2 tog, yfd, k1, yfd, sl 1, k1, psso, k9, mst 13; rep from * to end.
6th and every alt row: As 2nd row.
7th row: Mst 13, * k10, yfd, sl 1, k2 tog, psso, yfd, k10, mst 13; rep from * to end.
9th row: Mst 13, * k6, k2 tog, yfd, k1, yfd, sl 1, k1, psso, k1, k2 tog, yfd, k1, yfd, sl 1, k1, psso, k6, mst 13; rep from * to end.
11th row: Mst 13, * k7, yfd, sl 1, k2 tog, psso, yfd, k3, yfd, sl 1, k2 tog, psso, yfd, k7, mst 13; rep from * to end.
13th row: Mst 13, * k3, k2 tog, (yfd, k1, yfd, sl 1, k1, psso, k1, k2 tog) twice, yfd, k1, yfd, sl 1, k1, psso, k3, mst 13; rep from * to end.
15th row: Mst 13, * k4, yfd, sl 1, k2 tog, psso, yfd, k1, k2 tog, yfd, k3, yfd, sl 1, k1, psso, k1, yfd, sl 1, k2 tog, psso, yfd, k4, mst 13; rep from * to end.
17th row: Mst 13, * k2 tog, yfd, k1, yfd, sl 1, k1, psso, k2, k2 tog, yfd, k5, yfd, sl 1, k1, psso, k2, k2 tog, yfd, k1, yfd, sl 1, k1, psso, mst 13; rep from * to end.
19th row: Mst 13, * k1, yfd, sl 1, k2 tog, psso, yfd, k4, yfd, sl 1, k1, psso, k3, k2 tog, yfd, k4, yfd, sl 1, k2 tog, psso, yfd, k1, mst 13; rep from * to end.
21st row: Mst 13, * k3, k2 tog, (yfd, k1) twice, sl 1, k1, psso, yfd, sl 1, k1, psso, k1, k2 tog, yfd, k2 tog, (k1, yfd) twice, sl 1, k1, psso, k3, mst 13; rep from * to end.
23rd row: Mst 13, * k4, (yfd, sl 1, k2 tog, psso, yfd, k3) 3

times, k1, mst 13; rep from * to end.
25th row: As 9th row.
27th row: As 11th row.
29th row: As 5th row.
31st row: As 7th row.
33rd row: As 1st row.
34th row: As 2nd row.
35th to 48th row: Moss stitch.

Repeat rows 1-48 twice.

Cast off loosely and crochet a picot edge around the tray cloth as follows:
1st rnd: Work dc evenly around knitting with 3 dc in each corner.
2nd rnd: * 1 ss into next dc, 3 ch, 2 tr in same dc, miss next 2 dc; rep from * to end, 1 ss in 1st ss.
Cut yarn and work in yarn end. Damp, pin out to size and leave to dry.

Tea cosy

Instructions

For one side of tea cosy: Cast on 121 sts and work 14 rows in mst for border.
1st row: K25, * (p1, k1) 4 times, k24; rep from * to end.
2nd row: K1, p23, * (k1, p1) 4 times, k1, p23; rep from * to last st, k1.
3rd row: As 1st row.
4th and every alt row: As 2nd row.
5th row: K1, * k9, k2 tog, yfd, k1, yfd, sl 1, k1, psso, k9, mst 9 ; rep from * to last st and end with k1 instead of moss 9.
7th row: K1, * k10, yfd, sl 1, k2 tog, psso, yfd, k10, mst 9; rep from * to last st, k1 instead of moss 9.
9th row: K1, * k6, k2 tog, yfd, k1, yfd, sl 1, k1, psso, k1, k2 tog, yfd, k1, yfd, sl 1, k1, psso, k6, mst 9; rep from * to last st, k1 instead of moss 9.
11th row: K1, * k7, yfd, sl 1, k2 tog, psso, yfd, k3, yfd, sl 1, k2 tog, psso, yfd, k7, mst 9; rep from * to last st, k1 instead of moss 9.
13th row: K1, * k3, k2 tog, (yfd, k1, yfd, sl 1, k1, psso, k1, k2 tog) twice, yfd, k1, yfd, sl 1, k1, psso, k3, mst 9; rep from * to last st, k1 instead of moss 9.
15th row: K1, * k4, yfd, sl 1, k2 tog, psso, yfd, k1, k2 tog, yfd, k3, yfd, sl 1, k1, psso, k1, yfd, sl 1, k2 tog, psso, yfd, k4, mst 9; rep from * to last st, k1 instead of moss 9.
17th row: K1, * k2 tog, yfd, k1, yfd, sl 1, k1, psso, k2, k2 tog, yfd, k5, yfd, sl 1, k1, psso, k2, k2 tog, yfd, k1, yfd, sl 1, k1,

psso, mst 9; rep from * to last st, k1 instead of moss 9.

19th row: K1, * k1, yfd, sl 1, k2 tog, psso, yfd, k4, yfd, sl 1, k1, psso, k3, k2 tog, yfd, k4, yfd, sl 1, k2 tog, psso, yfd, k1, mst 9; rep from * to last st, k1 instead of moss 9.

21st row: K1, * k3, k2 tog, (yfd, k1) twice, sl 1, k1, psso, yfd, sl 1, k1, psso, k1, k2 tog, yfd, k2 tog, (k1, yfd) twice, sl 1, k1, psso, k3, mst 9; rep from * to last st, k1 instead of moss 9.

23rd row: K1, * k4, (yfd, sl 1, k2 tog, psso, yfd, k3) 3 times, k1, mst 9; rep from *6 to last st, k1 instead of mst 9.

25th row: As 9th row.

27th row: As 11th row.

29th row: As 5th row.

31st row: As 7th row.

33rd row: As 1st row.

34th row: As 2nd row.

35th to 48th row: Moss stitch.

Repeat rows 1-48 once. Now work the first and last squares in stocking st, retaining the pattern in the two centre squares only. Begin shaping the sides as follows: Dec 1 st at the beg and end of the next 2 rows, then work 3rd row without dec. Rep these 3 rows, retaining the pattern in the two centre squares until 34 rows have been completed. Cast off.

Knit the second side of the tea cosy in the same way.

Gusset: Cast on 15 sts and work 72 cm in mst (or until gusset is long enough to fit around the shaped edge of the tea cosy). Cast off.

Damp all the pieces, pin out to size and leave to dry. Sew the two sides of the tea cosy to the gusset and crochet the same picot edge as for tray cloth over these two seams.

Make a double lining for the tea cosy with a layer of batting in between. Place the lining inside the cosy and sew the knitting to the lining along the bottom edge, using slip stitches.

Round tablecloth, centrepiece and doily

Materials

12 × 50 g Tridalia crochet cotton no. 5 for tablecloth
2 × 50 g Tridalia crochet cotton no. 5 for centrepiece
1 × 50 g Tridalia crochet cotton no. 5 for doily.
4 double-pointed 2,50 mm knitting needles: 30 cm long
2,50 mm circular knitting needle: 80 cm long
2,50 mm circular knitting needle: 120 cm long
2,00 mm crochet hook

Size: Tablecloth; 160 cm in diameter; centrepiece: 55 cm in diameter; doily: 35 cm in diameter

Abbreviations: cr2 – cross 2 stitches = knit into front of 2nd st, then knit into front of 1st st and sl both sts off; cr3 – cross 3 stitches = sl 1, k2, psso; m1 – make 1 stitch = knit into front and back of next st

Tablecloth

Instructions

Cast on 8 sts and divide onto 3 needles (3, 3, 2). Form a circle and knit 2 rnds tbl.
The number of sts in each rnd is indicated in brackets at the end of the rnd except where the number of sts in consecutive rnds remains the same.
3rd rnd: * Yfd, k1 tbl; rep from * to end (= 16 sts).
4th and every alt rnd: Knit, but k tbl all sts worked tbl in previous rnd.
5th rnd: * Yfd, k1 tbl; rep from * to end (= 32 sts).
7th rnd: * Yfd, k2 tog, k1, yfd, k1 tbl; rep from * to end (= 40 sts).
9th rnd: * Yfd, k4, yfd, k1 tbl; rep from * to end (= 56 sts).
11th rnd: * Yfd, k2 tog, k2, sl 1, k1, psso, yfd, k1 tbl; rep from * to end.
13th rnd: * Yfd, k6, yfd, k1 tbl; rep from * to end (= 72 sts).
15th rnd: * Yfd, k2, k2 tog, yrn twice, sl 1, k1, psso, k2, yfd, k1 tbl; rep from * to end (= 88 sts).
16th and every alt rnd: As 4th rnd, but p1, k1 into each "yrn twice" of previous rnd.
17th rnd: * Yfd, k1, (k2 tog, yrn twice, sl 1, k1, psso) twice, k1, yfd, k1 tbl; rep from * to end (= 104 sts).
19th rnd: * Yfd, k2, (yrn twice, sl 1, k1, psso, k2 tog) twice, yrn twice, k2, yfd, k1 tbl; rep from * to end (= 136 sts).
21st rnd: * (K2 tog, yrn twice, sl 1, k1, psso) 4 times, k1 tbl; rep from * to end.
23rd rnd: * K2, (k2 tog, yrn twice, sl 1, k1, psso) 3 times, k2, yfd, k1 tbl, yfd; rep from * to end (= 152 sts).
25th rnd: * Sl 1, k1, psso, k2, (k2 tog, yrn twice, sl 1, k1, psso) twice, k2, k2 tog, yfd, sl 1, k2 tog, psso, yfd; rep from * to end (= 136 sts).
27th rnd: * K5, k2 tog, yrn twice, sl 1, k1, psso, k5, yfd, k3, yfd; rep from * to end (= 152 sts).
29th rnd: * Sl 1, k1, psso, k10, k2 tog, yfd, k2 tog, yfd, cr3, yfd; rep from * to end (= 144 sts).
30th and every alt rnd: As 4th rnd.
31st rnd: * K12, yfd, k1 tbl, yfd, cr3, yfd, k2 tog tbl, yfd; rep from * to end (= 160 sts).
33rd rnd: * Sl 1, k1, psso, k8, k2 tog, yfd, k1 tbl, (yfd, cr3) twice, yfd, k1 tbl, yfd; rep from * to end (= 168 sts).
35th rnd: * K10, yfd, k1 tbl, (yfd, cr3) 3 times, yfd, k1 tbl, yfd; rep from * to end (= 192 sts).
37th rnd: * Sl 1, k1, psso, k6, k2 tog, yfd, k1 tbl, (yfd, cr3) 4 times, yfd, k1 tbl, yfd; rep from * to end (= 200 sts).
39th rnd: * K8, yfd, k1 tbl, (yfd, cr3) 5 times, yfd, k1 tbl, yfd; rep from * to end (= 224 sts).
41st rnd: * Sl 1, k1, psso, k4, k2 tog, yfd, k1 tbl, (yfd, cr3) 6 times, yfd, k1 tbl, yfd; rep from * to end (= 232 sts).
43rd rnd: * K6, yfd, k1 tbl, (yfd, cr3) 7 times, yfd, k1 tbl, yfd; rep from * to end (= 256 sts).
45th rnd: * Sl 1, k1, psso, k2, k2 tog, yfd, k1 tbl, (yfd, cr3) 8 times, yfd, k1 tbl, yfd; rep from * to end (= 264 sts).
47th rnd: * K4, yfd, k1 tbl, (yfd, cr3) 9 times, yfd, k1 tbl, yfd; rep from * to end (= 288 sts).
49th rnd: * Sl 1, k1, psso, k2 tog, yfd, k1 tbl, (yfd, cr3) 10 times, yfd, k1 tbl, yfd; rep from * to end (= 296 sts).
51st rnd: * Yfd, k2 tog, yfd, k1 tbl, (yfd, cr3) 11 times, yfd, k1 tbl; rep from * to end (= 312 sts).
The number of sts in each rep and the total number of sts in the rnd are given in brackets at the end of each rnd.
53rd rnd: * K2 tog, k1 tbl, (yfd, cr3) 12 times, yfd; rep from * to end (= 39; 312 sts).
Change to 80 cm circular needle.
54th rnd: * Transfer 20 sts from left to right and mark new beg of rnd. Work as 4th rnd.
55th rnd: * Yfd, k1 tbl, yfd, k1, (cr3, yfd) 11 times, cr3, k1; rep from * to end (= 40; 320 sts).
57th rnd: * Yfd, k3, yfd, sl 1, k1, psso, (cr3, yfd) 10 times, cr3, k2 tog; rep from * to end (= 39; 312 sts).
59th rnd: * Yfd, k5, yfd, sl 1, k1, psso, (cr3, yfd) 9 times, cr3, k2 tog; rep from * to end (= 38; 304 sts).
61st rnd: * Yfd, k7, yfd, sl 1, k1, psso, (cr3, yfd) 8 times, cr3, k2 tog; rep from * to end (= 37; 296 sts).
63rd rnd: * Yfd, k9, yfd, sl 1, k1, psso, (cr3, yfd) 7 times, cr3, k2 tog; rep from * to end (= 36; 288 sts).
65th rnd: * Yfd, k5, yfd, k1 tbl, yfd, k5, yfd, sl 1, k1, psso, (cr3, yfd) 6 times, cr3, k2 tog; rep from * to end (= 37; 296 sts).

67th rnd: * Yfd, k6, yfd, k3, yfd, k6, yfd, sl 1, k1, psso, (cr3, yfd) 5 times, cr3, k2 tog; rep from * to end (= 38; 304 sts).

69th rnd: * Yfd, k7, yfd, k2, yrn twice, sl 1, k1, psso, k1, yfd, k7, yfd, sl 1, k1, psso, (cr3, yfd) 4 times, cr3, k2 tog; rep from * to end (= 40; 320 sts).

70th and every alt rnd: As 16th rnd.

71st rnd: * Yfd, k8, yfd, k2, yrn twice, sl 1, k1, psso, k2 tog, yrn twice, k2, yfd, k8, yfd, sl 1, k1, psso, (cr3, yfd) 3 times, cr3, k2 tog; rep from * to end (= 43; 344 sts).

73rd rnd: * Yfd, k9, yfd, k2, (yrn twice, sl 1, k1, psso, k2 tog) twice, yrn twice, k2, yfd, k9, yfd, sl 1, k1, psso, (cr3, yfd) twice, cr3, k2 tog; rep from * to end (= 46; 368 sts).

75th rnd: * Yfd, k10, yfd, k2, (yrn twice, sl 1, k1, psso, k2 tog) 3 times, yrn twice, k2, yfd, k10, yfd, sl 1, k1, psso, cr3, yfd, cr3, k2 tog; rep from * to end (= 49; 392 sts).

77th rnd: * Yfd, k11, yfd, k2, (yrn twice, sl 1, k1, psso, k2 tog) 4 times, yrn twice, k2, yfd, k11, yfd, sl 1, k1, psso, cr3, k2 tog; rep from * to end (= 52; 416 sts).

79th rnd: Transfer 12 sts from left to right, * yfd, k2, (yrn twice, sl 1, k1, psso, k2 tog) 5 times, yrn twice, k2, yfd, k12, yfd, sl 1, k1, psso, k2 tog, yfd, k12; rep from * to end (= 56; 448 sts).

81st rnd: * Yfd, k4, (k2 tog, yrn twice, sl 1, k1, psso) 5 times, k4, yfd, k10, yfd, k3, yfd, cr2, yfd, k3, yfd, k10; rep from * to end (= 62; 496 sts).

83rd rnd: * Yfd, k7, (k2 tog, yrn twice, sl 1, k1, psso) 4 times, k7, yfd, k11, yfd, k10, yfd, k11; rep from * to end (= 66; 528 sts).

85th rnd: * Yfd, k10, (k2 tog, yrn twice, sl 1, k1, psso) 3 times, k10, yfd, k12, yfd, sl 1, k1, psso, k6, k2 tog, yfd, k12; rep from * to end (= 68; 544 sts).

87th rnd: * Yfd, k13, (k2 tog, yrn twice, sl 1, k1, psso) twice, (k13, yfd) twice, sl 1, k1, psso, k4, k2 tog, yfd, k13; rep from * to end (= 70; 560 sts).

89th rnd: * K16, k2 tog, yrn twice, sl 1, k1, psso, k16, yfd, k14, yfd, sl 1, k1, psso, k2, k2 tog, yfd, k14, yfd; rep from * to end (= 72; 576 sts).

91st rnd: * Sl 1, k1, psso, k32, k2 tog, yfd, k1 tbl, yfd, k15, yfd, sl 1, k1, psso, k2 tog, yfd, k15, yfd, k1 tbl, yfd; rep from * to end (= 74; 592 sts).

92nd and every alt rnd: As 4th rnd.

93rd rnd: * Sl 1, k1, psso, k30, k2 tog, yfd, k3, yfd; rep from * to end (= 37; 592 sts)

95th rnd: * Sl 1, k1, psso, k28, k2 tog, yfd, k5, yfd; rep from * to end.

97th rnd: * Sl 1, k1, psso, k26, k2 tog, yfd, k1, k2 tog, yfd, k1 tbl, yfd, sl 1, k1, psso, k1, yfd; rep from * to end.

99th rnd: * Sl 1, k1, psso, k24, k2 tog, yfd, k2, k2 tog, yfd, k1 tbl, yfd, sl 1, k1, psso, k2, yfd; rep from * to end.

101st rnd: * Sl 1, k1, psso, k22, k2 tog, yfd, k3, k2 tog, yfd, k1 tbl, yfd, sl 1, k1, psso, k3, yfd; rep from * to end.

103rd rnd: * Sl 1, k1, psso, k20, k2 tog, yfd, k4, k2 tog, yfd, k1 tbl, yfd, sl 1, k1, psso, k4, yfd; rep from * to end.

105th rnd: * Sl 1, k1, psso, k18, k2 tog, yfd, k4, k2 tog, yfd, k3, yfd, sl 1, k1, psso, k4, yfd; rep from * to end.

107th rnd: * Sl 1, k1, psso, k16, k2 tog, yfd, k4, k2 tog, yfd,

sl 1, k1, psso, yfd, k1 tbl, yfd, k2 tog, yfd, sl 1, k1, psso, k4, yfd; rep from * to end.

109th rnd: * Sl 1, k1, psso, k14, k2 tog, yfd, k4, k2 tog, yfd, sl 1, k1, psso, yfd, sl 1, k2 tog, psso, yfd, k2 tog, yfd, sl 1, k1, psso, k4, yfd; rep from * to end (= 35; 560 sts).

111th rnd: * Sl 1, k1, psso, k12, k2 tog, yfd, k4, k2 tog, yfd, sl 1, k1, psso, yfd, k3, yfd, k2 tog, yfd, sl 1, k1, psso, k4, yfd; rep from * to end.

113th rnd: * Sl 1, k1, psso, k10, k2 tog, yfd, k4, k2 tog, yfd, sl 1, k1, psso, yfd, k5, yfd, k2 tog, yfd, sl 1, k1, psso, k4, yfd; rep from * to end.

115th rnd: * Sl 1, k1, psso, k8, k2 tog, yfd, k4, k2 tog, (yfd, k1 tbl) twice, yfd, sl 1, k1, psso, k3, k2 tog, (yfd, k1 tbl) twice, yfd, sl 1, k1, psso, k4, yfd; rep from * to end (= 37; 592 sts).

117th rnd: * Sl 1, k1, psso, k6, k2 tog, yfd, k4, k2 tog, yfd, sl 1, k1, psso, yfd, k3, yfd, sl 1, k1, psso, k1, k2 tog, yfd, k3, yfd, k2 tog, yfd, sl 1, k1, psso, k4, yfd; rep from * to end.

119th rnd: * Sl 1, k1, psso, (k4, k2 tog, yfd) twice, sl 1, k1, psso, yfd, k5, yfd, sl 1, k2 tog, psso, yfd, k5, yfd, k2 tog, yfd, sl 1, k1, psso, k4, yfd; rep from * to end.

121st rnd: * Sl 1, k1, psso, k2, k2 tog, yfd, k4, k2 tog, yfd, k1 tbl, (yfd, k1 tbl, yfd, sl 1, k1, psso, k3, k2 tog) twice, (yfd, k1 tbl) twice, yfd, sl 1, k1, psso, k4, yfd; rep from * to end (= 39; 624 sts).

123rd rnd: * Sl 1, k1, psso, k2 tog, yfd, k4, k2 tog, yfd, sl 1, k1, psso, (yfd, k3, yfd, sl 1, k1, psso, k1, k2 tog) twice, yfd, k3, yfd, k2 tog, yfd, sl 1, k1, psso, k4, yfd; rep from * to end.

125th rnd: Transfer 1 sts from left to right, * yfd, k5, k2 tog, yfd, sl 1, k1, psso, (yfd, k5, yfd, sl 1, k2 tog, psso) twice, yfd, k5, yfd, k2 tog, yfd, sl 1, k1, psso, k5; rep from * to end (= 40; 640 sts).

127th rnd: * K5, k2 tog, yfd, k1 tbl, (yfd, k1 tbl, yfd, sl 1, k1, psso, k3, k2 tog) 3 times, (yfd, k1 tbl) twice, yfd, sl 1, k1, psso, k4; rep from * to end (= 42; 672 sts).

129th rnd: * K4, k2 tog, yfd, sl 1, k1, psso, (yfd, k3, yfd, sl 1, k1, psso, k1, k2 tog) 3 times, yfd, k3, yfd, k2 tog, yfd, sl 1, k1, psso, k3; rep from * to end.

131st rnd: * K3, k2 tog, yfd, sl 1, k1, psso, (yfd, k5, yfd, sl 1, k2 tog, psso) 3 times, yfd, k5, yfd, k2 tog, yfd, sl 1, k1, psso, k2; rep from * to end.

133rd rnd: * K2, k2 tog, yfd, k1 tbl, (yfd, k1 tbl, yfd, sl 1, k1, psso, k3, k2 tog) 4 times, (yfd, k1 tbl) twice, yfd, sl 1, k1, psso, k1; rep from * to end (= 44; 704 sts).

135th rnd: * K1, k2 tog, yfd, sl 1, k1, psso, (yfd, k3, yfd, sl 1, k1, psso, k1, k2 tog) 4 times, yfd, k3, yfd, k2 tog, yfd, sl 1, k1, psso; rep from * to end.

136th rnd: Work to last st and mark new beg of rnd here.

137th rnd: * Sl 1, k2 tog, psso, yfd, sl 1, k1, psso, (yfd, k5, yfd, sl 1, k2 tog, psso) 4 times, yfd, k5, yfd, k2 tog, yfd; rep from * to end.

138th and every alt rnd: As 4th rnd.

139th rnd: * K1 tbl, yfd, sl 1, k1, psso, (yfd, sl 1, k1, psso, k3, k2 tog, yfd, k1 tbl) 4 times, yfd, sl 1, k1, psso, k3, (k2 tog, yfd) twice; rep from * to end.

141st rnd: * K1 tbl, yfd, k3, yfd, (sl 1, k1, psso, k1, k2 tog, yfd, k3, yfd) 5 times; rep from * to end (= 46; 736 sts).

143rd rnd: * K1 tbl, yfd, k5, yfd, (sl 1, k2 tog, psso, yfd, k5, yfd) 5 times; rep from * to end (= 48; 768 sts).

145th rnd: * Yfd, k1 tbl, yfd, sl 1, k1, psso, k3, k2 tog; rep from * to end.

147th rnd: * Yfd, k3, yfd, sl 1, k1, psso, k1, k2 tog; rep from * to end.

149th rnd: * Yfd, k5, yfd, sl 1, k2 tog, psso; rep from * to end.

151st rnd: * Sl 1, k1, psso, k3, k2 tog, yfd, k1 tbl, yfd; rep from * to end.

153rd rnd: * Sl 1, k1, psso, k1, k2 tog, yfd, k3, yfd; rep from * to end.

155th rnd: * Sl 1, k2 tog, psso, yfd, k5, yfd; rep from * to end.

156th rnd: Knit.

157th to 204th rnd: Rep 145th to 156th rnd 4 times (= 48; 768 sts).

Change to 120 cm circular needle.

205th rnd: Transfer 13 sts from left to right, * yfd, k3, (yfd, k1 tbl, yfd, sl 1, k1, psso, k3, k2 tog) twice, yfd, k1 tbl, yfd, k3, yfd, k1 tbl; rep from * to end (= 28; 896 sts).

207th rnd: * K5, (yfd, sl 1, k1, psso) twice, k1, k2 tog, yfd, k3, yfd, sl 1, k1, psso, k1, (k2 tog, yfd) twice, k5, yfd, k1 tbl, yfd; rep from * to end (= 30; 960 sts).

209th rnd: * Sl 1, k1, psso, k4, yfd, sl 1, k1, psso, yfd, sl 1, k2 tog, psso, yfd, k5, yfd, sl 1, k2 tog, psso, yfd, k2 tog, yfd, k4, k2 tog, yfd, k3, yfd; rep from * to end.

211th rnd: * Sl 1, k1, psso, k4, yfd, sl 1, k2 tog, psso, yfd, sl 1, k1, psso, k3, k2 tog, yfd, sl 1, k2 tog, psso, yfd, k4, (k2 tog, yfd) twice, cr3, yfd; rep from * to end (= 27; 864 sts).

213th rnd: * Sl 1, k1, psso, k4, (yfd, sl 1, k1, psso) twice, k1, (k2 tog, yfd) twice, k4, k2 tog, yfd, k1 tbl, yfd, cr3, yfd, sl 1, k1, psso, yfd; rep from * to end.

215th rnd: * Sl 1, k1, psso, k4, yfd, sl 1, k1, psso, yfd, sl 1, k2 tog, psso, yfd, k2 tog, yfd, k4, k2 tog, yfd, k1 tbl, (yfd, cr3) twice, yfd, k1 tbl, yfd; rep from * to end (= 28; 896 sts).

217th rnd: * Sl 1, k1, psso, k4, yfd, sl 1, k1, psso, k1, k2 tog, yfd, k4, k2 tog, yfd, k1 tbl, (yfd, cr3) 3 times, yfd, k1 tbl, yfd; rep from * to end (= 29; 928 sts).

219th rnd: * Sl 1, k1, psso, k4, yfd, sl 1, k2 tog, psso, yfd, k4, k2 tog, yfd, k1 tbl, (yfd, cr3) 4 times, yfd, k1 tbl, yfd; rep from * to end (= 30; 960 sts).

221st rnd: * Sl 1, k1, psso, k9, k2 tog, yfd, k1 tbl, (yfd, cr3) 5 times, yfd, k1 tbl, yfd; rep from * to end (= 31; 992 sts).

223rd rnd: * Sl 1, k1, psso, k7, k2 tog, yfd, k1 tbl, (yfd, cr3) 6 times, yfd, k1 tbl, yfd; rep from * to end (= 32; 1024 sts).

225th rnd: * Sl 1, k1, psso, k5, k2 tog, yfd, k1 tbl, (yfd, cr3) 3 times, k1, yfd, k1 tbl, yfd, k1, (cr3, yfd) 3 times, k1 tbl, yfd; rep from * to end (= 34; 1088 sts).

227th rnd: * Sl 1, k1, psso, k3, k2 tog, yfd, k1 tbl, (yfd, cr3) 3 times, k2 tog, yfd, k3, yfd, sl 1, k1, psso, (cr3, yfd) 3 times, k1 tbl, yfd; rep from * to end.

229th rnd: * Sl 1, k1, psso, k1, k2 tog, yfd, k1 tbl, (yfd, cr3) 3 times, k2 tog, yfd, k5, yfd, sl 1, k1, psso, (cr3, yfd) 3 times, k1 tbl, yfd; rep from * to end.

231st rnd: * Sl 1, k2 tog, psso, yfd, k1 tbl, (yfd, cr3) 3 times, k2 tog, yfd, k7, yfd, sl 1, k1, psso, (cr3, yfd) 3 times, k1 tbl, yfd; rep from * to end.

233rd rnd: * K1 tbl, yfd, k1 tbl, (yfd, cr3) 3 times, k2 tog, yfd, k9, yfd, sl 1, k1, psso, (cr3, yfd) 3 times, k1 tbl, yfd; rep from * to end (= 36; 1152 sts).

235th rnd: Transfer 13 sts from left to right and work as 65th round (= 37; 1184 sts).

237th rnd: As 67th rnd (= 38; 1216 sts).

239th rnd: As 69th rnd (= 40; 1280 sts).

240th and every alt rnd: As 16th rnd.

241st rnd: As 71st rnd (= 43; 1376 sts).

243rd rnd: As 73rd rnd (= 46; 1472 sts).

245th rnd: As 75th rnd (= 49; 1568 sts).

247th rnd: As 77th rnd (= 52; 1664 sts).

From here onwards the figure in square brackets at the end of each rnd indicates the number of sts per rnd for the centrepiece.

249th rnd: * K10, k2 tog, yfd, sl 1, k1, psso, (yrn twice, sl 1, k1, psso, k2 tog) 5 times, yrn twice, k2 tog, yfd, sl 1, k1, psso, k10, yfd, sl 1, k1, psso, k2 tog, yfd; rep from * to end (= 52; 1664 [416] sts).

251st rnd: * K9, k2 tog, yfd, k1 tbl, yfd, sl 1, k1, psso, k4, (k2 tog, yrn twice, sl 1, k1, psso) 3 times, k4, k2 tog, yfd, k1 tbl, yfd, sl 1, k1, psso, k9, sl 1, k1, psso, k2 tog; rep from * to end (= 50; 1600 [400] sts).

253rd rnd: * K8, k2 tog, yfd, sl 1, k2 tog, psso, yfd, sl 1, k1, psso, k5, (k2 tog, yrn twice, sl 1, k1, psso) twice, k5, k2 tog, yfd, sl 1, k2 tog, psso, yfd, sl 1, k1, psso, k10; rep from * to end (= 46; 1472 [368] sts).

255th rnd: * K7, k2 tog, yfd, k3, yfd, sl 1, k1, psso, k6, k2 tog, yrn twice, sl 1, k1, psso, k6, k2 tog, yfd, k3, yfd, sl 1, k1, psso, k9; rep from * to end.

257th rnd: Transfer 8 sts from left to right, * yfd, sl 1, k1, psso, yfd, k1 tbl, yfd, k2 tog, yfd, sl 1, k1, psso, k14, k2 tog; rep from * to end.

258th and every alt rnd: As 4th rnd.

259th rnd: * Yfd, sl 1, k1, psso, yfd, sl 1, k2 tog, psso, yfd, k2 tog, yfd, sl 1, k1, psso, k12, k2 tog; rep from * to end (= 21; 1344 [336] sts).

261st rnd: * Yfd, sl 1, k1, psso, yrn twice, sl 1, k2 tog, psso, yrn twice, k2 tog, yfd, sl 1, k1, psso, k10, k2 tog; rep from * to end.

262nd and every alt rnd: As 16th rnd.

263rd rnd: * Yfd, (k3, yrn twice) twice, k3, yfd, sl 1, k1, psso, k8, k2 tog; rep from * to end (= 25; 1600 [400] sts).

265th rnd: * Yfd, (sl 1, k1, psso, k1, k2 tog, yrn twice) twice, sl 1, k1, psso, k1, k2 tog, yfd, sl 1, k1, psso, k6, k2 tog; rep from * to end (= 23; 1472 [368] sts).

267th rnd: * Yfd, (k5, yrn twice) twice, k5, yfd, sl 1, k1, psso, k4, k2 tog; rep from * to end (= 27; 1728 [432] sts).

269th rnd: * Yfd, (k1, k2 tog, m1, sl 1, k1, psso, k1, yrn twice) twice, k1, k2 tog, m1, sl 1, k1, psso, k1, yfd, sl 1, k1, psso, k2, k2 tog; rep from * to end (= 28; 1792 [448] sts).

271st rnd: * (Yfd, k1, k2 tog, yfd, k2, yfd, sl 1, k1, psso, k1) 3 times, yfd, sl 1, k1, psso, k2 tog; rep from * to end (= 30; 1920 [480] sts).

272nd rnd: Knit.

Crochet sts off as follows: * 1 dc into next 3 sts, 12 ch, 1 dc into next 4 sts, 12 ch, (1 dc into next 5 sts, 12 ch, 1 dc into next 4 sts, 12 ch) twice, 1 dc into next 3 sts, 12 ch, 1 dc into next 2 sts, 12 ch; rep from * to end, 1 ss into 1st dc.

Cut yarn and work in yarn end. Damp, pin out to size and leave to dry.

Centrepiece

Instructions

Cast on 8 sts and work as tablecloth for 78 rnds (= 416 sts). Keep work on 80 cm circular needle. Now work 249th to 272nd rnds of tablecloth.

Crochet sts off as for tablecloth.

Damp, pin out to size and leave to dry.

Doily

Instructions

Cast on 8 sts and work as tablecloth for 51 rnds. Knit 3 rnds (= 312 sts).

Crochet sts off as follows: * 1 dc into next 3 sts, 6 ch; rep from * to end, 1 ss into 1st dc.

Cut yarn and work in yarn end. Damp, pin out to size and leave to dry.

Tray cloth with diamond motif

Materials

1 x 50 gr Tridalia crochet cotton no. 8
5 double-pointed 2,50 mm knitting needles: 30 cm long
2,50 mm circular knitting needle: 80 cm long
1,50 mm crochet hook

Size: 45 cm × 33 cm

Abbreviations: p2sso = pass 2 slipped stitches over

Instructions

Cast on 64 sts (16 sts on each of 4 needles). Form a circle and knit 1 rnd.
1st rnd: * K1 tbl, yfd, (k15, yfd) twice, k1 tbl, yfd; rep from * to end.
2nd and every alt rnd: Knit.
3rd rnd: * K1 tbl, yfd, k1, (yfd, sl 1, k1, psso, k11, k2 tog, yfd, k1) twice, yfd, k1 tbl, yfd, k1, yfd; rep from * to end.
5th rnd: * K1 tbl, yfd, k2, (k1, yfd, sl 1, k1, psso, k9, k2 tog, yfd, k2) twice, k1, yfd, k1 tbl, yfd, k3, yfd; rep from * to end.
7th rnd: * K1 tbl, yfd, k3, (k2, yfd, sl 1, k1, psso, k7, k2 tog, yfd, k3) twice, k2, yfd, k1 tbl, yfd, k5, yfd; rep from * to end.
9th rnd: * K1 tbl, yfd, k4, (k3, yfd, sl 1, k1, psso, k5, k2 tog, yfd, k4) twice, k3, yfd, k1 tbl, yfd, k7, yfd; rep from * to end.
11th rnd: * K1 tbl, yfd, k5, (k4, yfd, sl 1, k1, psso, k3, k2 tog, yfd, k5) twice, k4, yfd, k1 tbl, yfd, k9, yfd; rep from * to end.
13th rnd: * K1 tbl, yfd, k6, (k5, yfd, sl 1, k1, psso, k1, k2 tog, yfd k6) twice, k5, yfd, k1 tbl, yfd, k11, yfd; rep from * to end.
15th rnd: * K1 tbl, yfd, k7, (k6, yfd, sl 1, k2 tog, psso, yfd, k7) twice, k6, yfd, k1 tbl, yfd, k13, yfd; rep from * to end.
17th rnd: * K1 tbl, yfd, k1, yfd, k7, (k6, yfd, sl 1, k2 tog, psso, yfd, k7) twice, k6, yfd, k1, yfd, k1 tbl, yfd, k1, yfd, k13, yfd, k1, yfd; rep from * to end.
19th rnd: * K1 tbl, yfd, k2, ** k1, yfd, k5, sl 1, k2 tog, psso, k5, yfd, k2 **; rep twice from ** to **, k1, yfd, k1 tbl, yfd, k2; rep once from ** to **, k1, yfd; rep from * to end.
21st rnd: * K1 tbl, yfd, k1, yfd, sl 1, k2 tog, psso, ** yfd, k1, yfd, k4, sl 1, k2 tog, psso, k4, yfd, k1, yfd, sl 1, k2 tog, psso **; rep twice from ** to **, yfd, k1, yfd, k1 tbl, yfd, k1, yfd, sl 1, k2 tog, psso; rep once from ** to **, yfd, k1, yfd; rep from * to end.
23rd rnd: * K1 tbl, yfd, k3, yfd, k1 tbl, ** (yfd, k3) twice, sl 1, k2 tog, psso, (k3, yfd) twice, k1 tbl **; rep twice from ** to **, (yfd, k3, yfd, k1 tbl) twice; rep once from ** to **, yfd, k3, yfd; rep from * to end.
25th rnd: * K1 tbl, yfd, k1, (yfd, sl 1, k2 tog, psso) twice, ** yfd, sl 1, k2 tog, psso, yfd, k1, yfd, k2, sl 1, k2 tog, psso, k2, yfd, k1, (yfd, sl 1, k2 tog, psso) twice **; rep twice from

** to **, yfd, sl 1, k2 tog, psso, yfd, k1, yfd, k1 tbl, yfd, k1, (yfd, sl 1, k2 tog, psso) twice; rep once from ** to **, yfd, sl 1, k2 tog, psso, yfd, k1, yfd; rep from * to end.
27th rnd: * K1 tbl, yfd, k3, yfd, k1 tbl, yfd, k2, ** k1, yfd, k1 tbl, yfd, k3, yfd, sl 2, k3 tog, p2sso, yfd, k3, yfd, k1 tbl, yfd, k2 **; rep twice from ** to **, k1, (yfd, k1 tbl, yfd, k3) twice, yfd, k1 tbl, yfd, k2; rep once from ** to **, k1, yfd, k1 tbl, yfd, k3, yfd; rep from * to end.
29th rnd: * K1 tbl, yfd, k1, (yfd, sl 1, k2 tog, psso) 23 times, yfd, k1, yfd, k1 tbl, yfd, k1, (yfd, sl 1, k2 tog, psso) 11 times, yfd, k1, yfd; rep from * to end.
Change to circular needle.
31st rnd: * (K1 tbl, yfd, k3, yfd) 20 times; rep from * to end.
33rd rnd: * K1 tbl, yfd, k1, (yfd, sl 1, k2 tog, psso) 25 times, yfd, k1, yfd, k1 tbl, yfd, k1, (yfd, sl 1, k2 tog, psso) 13 times, yfd, k1, yfd; rep from * to end.
35th rnd: * (K1 tbl, yfd, k3, yfd) 22 times; rep from * to end.
37th rnd: * K1 tbl, yfd, k1, (yfd, sl 1, k2 tog, psso) 27 times, yfd, k1, yfd, k1 tbl, yfd, k1, (yfd, sl 1, k2 tog, psso) 15 times, yfd, k1, yfd; rep from * to end.
39th rnd: * (K1 tbl, yfd, k3, yfd) 24 times; rep from * to end.
41st rnd: * K1 tbl, yfd, k1, (yfd, sl 1, k2 tog, psso) 29 times, yfd, k1, yfd, k1 tbl, yfd, k1, (yfd, sl 1, k2 tog, psso) 17 times, yfd, k1, yfd; rep from * to end.
43rd rnd: * K1 tbl, yfd, k2, ** k1, yfd, (k1 tbl, yfd, k3, yfd) twice, k1 tbl, yfd, k2 **; rep 4 times from ** to **, k1, yfd, k1 tbl, yfd, k2; rep 3 times from ** to **, k1, yfd; rep from * to end.
45th rnd: * K1 tbl, yfd, k3, ** k2, yfd, sl 1, k1, psso, (yfd, sl 1, k2 tog, psso) 3 times, yfd, k2 tog, yfd, k3 **; rep 4 times from ** to **, k2, yfd, k1 tbl, yfd, k3; rep 3 times from ** to **, k2, yfd; rep from * to end.
47th rnd: * K1 tbl, yfd, k4, ** k3, (yfd, sl 1, k1, psso) twice, k1, (k2 tog, yfd) twice, k4 **; rep 4 times from ** to **, k3, yfd, k1 tbl, yfd, k4; rep 3 times from ** to **, k3, yfd; rep from * to end.
49th rnd: * K1 tbl, yfd, k5, ** k4, yfd, sl 1, k1, psso, yfd, sl 1, k2 tog, psso, yfd, k2 tog, yfd, k5 **; rep 4 times from ** to **, k4, yfd, k1 tbl, yfd, k5; rep 3 times from ** to **, k4, yfd; rep from * to end.
51st rnd: * K1 tbl, yfd, k4, k2 tog, yrn 4 times, ** yrn 3 times, k5, yfd, sl 1, k1, psso, k1, k2 tog, yfd, k4, k2 tog, yrn 4 times **, rep 4 times from ** to **, yrn 3 times, k5, yfd, k1 tbl, yfd, k4, k2 tog, yrn 4 times; rep 3 times from ** to **, yrn 3 times, k5, yfd; rep from * to end.
52nd rnd: Knit, but work 7 sts (k1, p1, k1, p1, k1, p1, k1) in "yrn 4 times" and "yrn 3 times" of previous rnd.
53rd rnd: * K1 tbl, yfd, k10, ** k9, yfd, sl 1, k2 tog, psso, yfd, k10 **; rep 4 times from ** to **, k9, yfd, k1 tbl, yfd, k10; rep 3 times from ** to **, k9, yfd; rep from * to end.

55th rnd: * (K1 tbl, yfd, k21, yfd) 10 times; rep from * to end.
56th rnd: Knit.

Knit 2 sts and crochet sts off as follows: * (1 dc into next 3 sts, 10 ch) 6 times, (1 dc into next 3 sts, 4 ch) twice; rep 19 times from *, 1 ss into 1st dc.

Cut yarn and secure end with a few stitches into chain stitch loop.

Fold tray cloth in half lengthwise, with right sides facing, and sew up the opening in the centre. Match pattern carefully. Cut yarn and work in yarn end. Damp, pin out to size and leave to dry.

Knitted lace curtain

Materials

1 × 50 g Tridalia crochet cotton no. 8 (enough for 45 cm
width × 56 cm drop)
One pair 2,25 mm knitting needles: 30 cm long

Measurements: 56 cm drop × required width

Abbreviations: m1 – make one stitch = knit into front
and back of next st

Instructions

Cast on 153 sts and knit one row.
Knit all uneven rows, but k1, p1 into each "yfd" of previous
row.
2nd row: K1, k1 tbl, k1, (k2 tog, tbl) twice, yfd, (k2 tog tbl)
twice, yfd, k2 tog tbl, k3, k2 tog, yfd, k2 tog tbl, yfd, k2 tog
tbl, k3, k2 tog, yfd, k2 tog tbl, yfd, k2 tog tbl, k3, k2 tog, yfd,
(k2 tog tbl) twice, yfd, k2 tog tbl, k111.
4th row: K1, k1 tbl, k1, (k2 tog tbl) twice, yfd, (k2 tog tbl)
twice, yfd, k2 tog tbl, k1, k2 tog, yfd, k2 tog tbl, k1, k2 tog tbl,
yfd, k2 tog tbl, k1, k2 tog, yfd, k2 tog tbl, k1, k2 tog tbl, yfd,
k2 tog tbl, k1, k2 tog, yfd, (k2 tog tbl) twice, yfd, k2 tog tbl,
k103, k2 tog, yfd, k2 tog tbl, k5.
6th row: K1, k1 tbl, k1, (k2 tog tbl) twice, yfd, (k2 tog tbl)
twice, yfd, sl 1, k2 tog, psso, yfd, k2 tog tbl, k3, k2 tog tbl,
yfd, sl 1, k2 tog, psso, yfd, k2 tog tbl, k3, k2 tog tbl, yfd, sl
1, k2 tog, psso, yfd, (k2 tog tbl) twice, yfd, k2 tog tbl, k113.
8th row: K1, k1 tbl, k1, (k2 tog tbl) twice, yfd, (k2 tog tbl)
twice, yfd, sl 1, k2 tog, psso, k5, sl 1, k2 tog, psso, yfd, k2 tog
tbl, k5, sl 1, k2 tog, psso, yfd, (k2 tog tbl) twice, yfd, k2 tog
tbl, k105, k2 tog, yfd, k2 tog tbl, k5.
10th row: K1, k1 tbl, k1, (k2 tog tbl) twice, yfd, (k2 tog tbl)
twice, yfd, k2 tog tbl, k3, k2 tog, yfd, k2 tog tbl, yfd, k2 tog
tbl, k3, k2 tog, yfd, (k2 tog tbl) twice, yfd, k2 tog tbl, k115.
12th row: K1, k1 tbl, k1, (k2 tog tbl) twice, yfd, (k2 tog tbl)
twice, yfd, k2 tog tbl, k1, k2 tog, yfd, k2 tog tbl, k1, k2 tog tbl,
yfd, k2 tog tbl, k1, k2 tog, yfd, (k2 tog tbl) twice, yfd, k2 tog
tbl, k107, k2 tog, yfd, k2 tog tbl, k5.
14th row: K1, k1 tbl, k1, (k2 tog tbl) twice, yfd, (k2 tog tbl)
twice, yfd, sl 1, k2 tog, psso, yfd, k2 tog tbl, k3, k2 tog tbl,
yfd, sl 1, k2 tog, psso, yfd, (k2 tog tbl) twice, yfd, k2 tog tbl,
k2 tog, yfd, k2 tog tbl, (k10, k2 tog, yfd, k2 tog tbl) 7 times,
k15.
16th row: K1, k1 tbl, k1, (k2 tog tbl) twice, yfd, (k2 tog tbl)
twice, yfd, sl 1, k2 tog, psso, k5, sl 1, k2 tog, psso, yfd, (k2
tog tbl) twice, yfd, k2 tog tbl, k109, k2 tog, yfd, k2 tog tbl, k5.
18th row: K1, k1 tbl, k1, (k2 tog tbl) twice, yfd, (k2 tog tbl)
twice, yfd, k2 tog tbl, k3, k2 tog, yfd, (k2 tog tbl) twice, yfd,
k2 tog tbl, k2 tog, yfd, k2 tog tbl, k2 tog, yfd, k2 tog tbl, (k6,
k2 tog, yfd, k2 tog tbl, k2 tog, yfd, k2 tog tbl) 7 times, k13.
20th row: K1, k1 tbl, k1, (k2 tog tbl) twice, yfd, (k2 tog tbl)
twice, yfd, k2 tog tbl, k1, k2 tog, yfd, (k2 tog tbl) twice, yfd,
k2 tog tbl, k111, k2 tog, yfd, k2 tog tbl, k5.
22nd row: K1, k1 tbl, k1, (k2 tog tbl) twice, yfd, (k2 tog tbl)
twice, yfd, sl 1, k2 tog, psso, yfd, (k2 tog tbl) twice, yfd, k2
tog tbl, k2 tog, yfd, k2 tog tbl, k2 tog, yfd, k2 tog tbl, k2 tog,
yfd, k2 tog tbl, (k2, k2 tog, yfd, k2 tog tbl, k2 tog, yfd, k2 tog
tbl, k2 tog, yfd, k2 tog tbl) 7 times, k11.
24th row: K1, k1 tbl, m1, k2 tog tbl, yfd, (k2 tog tbl) twice,
yfd, k2 tog tbl, k1, k2 tog tbl, yfd, (k2 tog tbl) twice, yfd, k2
tog tbl, k111, k2 tog, yfd, k2 tog tbl, k5.
26th row: K1, k1 tbl, m1, k2 tog tbl, yfd, (k2 tog tbl) twice,
yfd, k2 tog tbl, k3, k2 tog tbl, yfd, (k2 tog tbl) twice, yfd, k2
tog tbl, k2 tog, yfd, k2 tog tbl, (k6, k2
tog, yfd, k2 tog tbl, k2 tog, yfd, k2 tog tbl) 7 times, k13.
28th row: K1, k1 tbl, m1, k2 tog tbl, yfd, (k2 tog tbl) twice,
yfd, k2 tog tbl, k5, k2 tog, yfd, (k2 tog tbl) twice, yfd, k2 tog
tbl, k109, k2 tog, yfd, k2 tog tbl, k5.
30th row: K1, k1 tbl, m1, k2 tog tbl, yfd, (k2 tog tbl) twice,
yfd, k2 tog tbl, yfd, k2 tog tbl, k3, k2 tog, yfd, k2 tog tbl, yfd,
(k2 tog tbl) twice, yfd, k2 tog tbl, k2 tog, yfd, (k10,
k2 tog, yfd, k2 tog tbl) 7 times, k15.
32nd row: K1, k1 tbl, m1, k2 tog tbl, yfd, (k2 tog tbl) twice,
yfd, k2 tog tbl, k1, k2 tog tbl, yfd, k2 tog tbl, k1, k2 tog, yfd,
k2 tog tbl, k1, k2 tog tbl, yfd, (k2 tog tbl) twice, yfd, k2 tog tbl,
k107, k2 tog, yfd, k2 tog tbl, k5.
34th row: K1, k1 tbl, m1, k2 tog tbl, yfd, (k2 tog tbl) twice,
yfd, k2 tog tbl, k3, k2 tog tbl, yfd, sl 1, k2 tog, psso, yfd, k2
tog tbl, k3, k2 tog tbl, yfd, (k2 tog tbl) twice, yfd, k2 tog tbl,
k115.
36th row: K1, k1 tbl, m1, k2 tog tbl, yfd, (k2 tog tbl) twice,
yfd, k2 tog tbl, k5, k2 tog, yfd, sl 1, k2 tog, psso, k5, k2 tog,
yfd, (k2 tog tbl) twice, yfd, k2 tog tbl, k105, k2 tog, yfd, k2 tog
tbl, k5.
38th row: K1, k1 tbl, m1, k2 tog tbl, yfd, (k2 tog tbl) twice,
yfd, k2 tog tbl, yfd, k2 tog tbl, k3, k2 tog, yfd, k2 tog tbl, yfd,
k2 tog tbl, k3, k2 tog, yfd, k2 tog tbl, yfd, (k2 tog tbl) twice,
yfd, k2 tog tbl, k113.
40th row: K1, k1 tbl, m1, k2 tog tbl, yfd, (k2 tog tbl) twice,
yfd, k2 tog tbl, k1, k2 tog tbl, yfd, k2 tog tbl, k1, k2 tog, yfd,
k2 tog tbl, k1, k2 tog tbl, yfd, k2 tog tbl, k1, k2 tog, yfd, k2 tog
tbl, k1, k2 tog tbl, yfd, (k2 tog tbl) twice, yfd, k2 tog tbl, k103,
k2 tog, yfd, k2 tog tbl, k5.
42nd row: K1, k1 tbl, m1, k2 tog tbl, yfd, (k2 tog tbl) twice,
yfd, k2 tog tbl, k3, k2 tog tbl, yfd, sl 1, k2 tog, psso, yfd, k2
tog tbl, k3, k2 tog tbl, yfd, sl 1, k2 tog, psso, yfd, k2 tog tbl,
k3, k2 tog tbl, yfd, (k2 tog tbl) twice, yfd, k2 tog tbl, k111.
44th row: K1, K1 tbl, m1, k2 tog tbl, yfd, (k2 tog tbl) twice,

yfd, k2 tog tbl, k5, sl 1, k2 tog, psso, yfd, k2 tog tbl, k5, sl 1, k2 tog, psso, yfd, k2 tog tbl, k5, k2 tog, yfd, (k2 tog tbl) twice, yfd, k2 tog tbl, k101, k2 tog, yfd, k2 tog tbl, k5.
45th row: Knit, but k1, p1 into each "yfd" of previous row.

Repeat rows 2-45 to required width and cast off.

Damp, pin out to size and leave to dry. Thread curtain wire through the top to hang the curtain.

Centrepiece with tulip motif

Materials

1 x 50 g Tridalia crochet cotton no. 8
4 double-pointed 2,50 mm knitting needles: 30 cm long
2,50 mm circular knitting needle: 80 cm long

Size: 44 cm in diameter

Instructions

Cast on 8 sts and divide onto 3 needles (3, 3, 2). Form a circle and knit 1st rnd.
The number of sts in each rnd is indicated in brackets at the end of the rnd, except where the number of sts in consecutive rnds remains the same.

2nd rnd: * K1 and p1 into next st; rep from * to end (= 16 sts).
3rd rnd: Knit.
4th rnd: As 2nd rnd (= 32 sts).
5th to 7th rnd: Knit.
8th rnd: As 2nd rnd (= 64 sts).
9th to 11th rnd: Knit.
12th rnd: * Yfd, sl 1, k1, psso, k4, k2 tog; rep from * to end (= 56 sts).
13th rnd: * (K1, p1) 3 times into each "yfd" of previous rnd, k6; rep from * to end (= 96 sts).
14th rnd: * K6 tbl, k6; rep from * to end (= 96 sts).
15th to 18th rnd: Knit. (= 96 sts).
19th rnd: Transfer 3 sts from left to right and mark new beg of rnd. When sts are transferred at the beg of a rnd, remember to adjust sts on other needles as well. * Yfd, k6; rep from * to end (= 112 sts).
20th rnd: Knit, but k1, p1 into each "yfd" of previous rnd (= 128 sts).
21st rnd: Transfer 1 st from left to right, * yfd, k1 tbl, k6, k1 tbl; rep from * to end (= 144 sts).
22nd rnd: As 20th rnd (= 160 sts).
23rd rnd: Transfer 1 st from left to right, * yfd, k1 tbl, k8, k1 tbl; rep from * to end (= 176 sts).
24th rnd: * (K1, p1) twice into each "yfd" of previous rnd, k10; rep from * to end (= 224 sts).
25th rnd: * Yfd, k4 tbl, yfd, (sl 1, k1, psso, k1, k2 tog) twice; rep from * to end (= 192 sts).
26th and every alt rnd unless otherwise stated: Knit, but k1, p1 into each "yfd" of previous rnd (= 224 sts).
27th rnd: Transfer 1 st from left to right, * yfd, k1 tbl, k4, k1 tbl, yfd, (sl 1, k1, psso, k2 tog) twice; rep from * to end (= 192 sts).
29th rnd: Transfer 1 st from left to right, * yfd, k1 tbl, k6, k1 tbl, yfd, (sl 1, k2 tog, psso) twice; rep from * to end

(= 192 sts).
31st rnd: Transfer 1 st from left to right, * yfd, k1 tbl, k8, k1 tbl, yfd, sl 1, k1, psso, k2 tog; rep from * to end (= 224 sts).
32nd rnd: As 26th rnd (= 256 sts).
33rd rnd: Transfer 1 st from left to right, * yfd, k1 tbl, k5, yfd, k5, k1 tbl, yfd, sl 1, k1, psso, k2 tog; rep from * to end (= 272 sts).
34th, 36th and 38th rnds: As 26th rnd (= 320 sts).
35th rnd: Transfer 1 st from right to left, * yfd, sl 1, k1, psso, k6, k2 tog; rep from * to end (= 288 sts).
37th rnd: Transfer 1 st from left to right. Work as 35th rnd from * to end (= 288 sts).
39th rnd: Transfer 1 st from left to right, * yfd, (sl 1, k1, psso, k1, k2 tog) twice; rep from * to end (= 224 sts).
40th rnd: As 26th rnd (= 256 sts).
41st rnd: Transfer 1 st from left to right, * yfd, (sl 1, k1, psso, k4, k2 tog) twice; rep from * to the end (= 208 sts).
42nd rnd: (K1, p1) 4 times into each "yfd" of previous rnd, k12; rep from * to end (= 320 sts).
43rd rnd: Transfer 1 st from left to right, * yfd, k6 tbl, yfd, (sl 1, k1, psso, k3, k2 tog) twice; rep from * to end (= 288 sts).
44th rnd: As 26th rnd (= 320 sts).
45th rnd: Transfer 1 st from left to right, * (yfd, sl 1, k1, psso) 4 times, yfd, (sl 1, k1, psso, k2, k2 tog) twice; rep from * to end (= 272 sts).
Change to circular knitting needle.
46th rnd: As 26th rnd (= 352 sts).
47th rnd: Transfer 1 st from left to right,* yrn twice, (sl 1, k2 tog, psso, yfd) 3 times, sl 1, k2 tog, psso, yrn twice, (sl 1, k1, psso, k1, k2 tog) twice; rep from * to end (= 272 sts).
48th rnd: Knit, but k1, p1 into each "yfd" of previous rnd and (k1, p1) twice into each "yrn twice" of previous rnd (= 384 sts).
49th rnd: Transfer 1 st from left to right, * yfd, k2 tbl, (yfd, sl 1, k2 tog, psso) 4 times, yfd, k2 tbl, yfd, (sl 1, k1, psso, k2 tog) twice; rep from * to end (= 304 sts).
50th rnd: K1, p1 into each "yfd" of previous rnd, * sl 1, k1, psso, knit 14 sts, but k1, p1 into each "yfd" of previous rnd. Where instructions follow to knit a specific number of sts, the 2 sts into each "yfd" are counted as 2 sts.
Sl 1, k1, psso, knit 8 sts, counting sts into "yfd" as before; rep from * to end. Finish last rep with k6 sts, counting sts into "yfd" as before (= 384 sts).
51st rnd: Transfer 1 st from left to right, * (yfd, sl 1, k2 tog, psso) 7 times, sl 1, k2 tog, psso; rep from * to end (= 240 sts).
52nd rnd: Knit 20 sts, but k1, p1 into each "yfd" of previous rnd, counting sts as before, k2 tog; rep from * to end (= 336 sts).

53rd and 55th rnd: Transfer 1 st from left to right, * yfd, sl 1, k2 tog, psso; rep from * to end (= 224 sts).

54th and 56th rnd: As 26th round (= 336 sts).

57th rnd: Transfer 1 st from left to right, (yfd, sl 1, k2 tog, psso) 3 times, * yrn twice, sl 1, k2 tog, psso, (yfd, sl 1, k2 tog, psso) 6 times; rep from * to last 12 sts, yrn twice, sl 1, k2 tog, psso, (yfd, sl 1, k2 tog, psso) 3 times (= 240 sts).

58th rnd: As 48th rnd (= 368 sts).

59th rnd: Transfer 1 st from left to right, * (yfd, sl 1, k2 tog, psso) 3 times, yfd, k2 tbl, (yfd, sl 1, k2 tog, psso) 4 times; rep from * to end (= 272 sts).

60th rnd: As 26th rnd (= 400 sts).

61st rnd: Transfer 1 st from left to right, * (yfd, sl 1, k2 tog, psso) twice, sl 1, k2 tog, psso, yfd, (k1, p1 into next sts) 4 times, yfd, (sl 1, k2 tog, psso) twice, (yfd, sl 1, k2 tog, psso) twice; rep from * to end (= 336 sts).

62nd rnd: Knit 5 sts, but k1, p1 into each "yfd" of previous rnd, counting sts as before, * k2 tog, knit 12 sts, counting sts into "yfd" as before, k2 tog, knit 11 sts, counting sts into "yfd" as before; rep from * to end. Finish last rep with knit 6 sts and count sts in "yfd" as before (= 400 sts).

63rd rnd: Transfer 1 st from left to right, * (yfd, sl 1, k2 tog, psso) twice, yfd, k1 tbl, k8, k1 tbl, (yfd, sl 1, k2 tog, psso) 3 times; rep from * to end (= 336 sts).

64th rnd: As 26th rnd (= 432 sts).

65th rnd: Transfer 4 sts from left to right, * yfd, sl 1, k2 tog, psso, yfd, k1 tbl, k10, k1 tbl, (yfd, sl 1, k2 tog, psso) twice, (sl 1, k2 tog, psso) twice; rep from * to end (= 336 sts).

66th rnd: * Knit 22 sts, but k1, p1 into each "yfd" of previous rnd, counting sts as before, sl 1, k2 tog, psso; rep from * to end (= 368 sts).

67th rnd: Transfer 1 st from left to right, * yfd, sl 1, k2 tog, psso, yfd, k1 tbl, k6, yfd, k6, k1 tbl, (yfd, sl 1, k2 tog, psso) twice; rep from * to end (= 352 sts).

68th rnd: As 26th rnd (= 432 sts).

69th rnd: Transfer 4 sts from left to right, * (yfd, sl 1, k1, psso, k5, k2 tog) twice, yfd, sl 1, k1, psso, k5 tbl, k2 tog; rep

from * to end (= 384 sts).

70th rnd: As 26th rnd (= 432 sts).

71st rnd: Transfer 1 st from left to right, * yrn twice, (sl 1, k1, psso) twice, k1, (k2 tog) twice; rep from * to end (= 336 sts).

72nd rnd: * (K1, p1) 4 times into each "yrn twice" of previous rnd, sl 1, k1, psso, k1, k2 tog; rep from * to end (= 528 sts).

73rd rnd: * K8 tbl, sl 1, k2 tog, psso; rep from * to end (= 432 sts).

Cast off loosely.

Damp, pin out to size and leave to dry.

Gossamer oval doily

Materials

1 × 50 g Tridalia crochet cotton no. 8
8 double-pointed 2,50 mm knitting needles: 30 cm long
2,25 mm crochet hook

Size: 50 cm × 35 cm

Abbreviations: m2 – make 2 stitches = k1, p1 and k1 into next st

Instructions

Cast on 96 sts (32 sts on each of 3 needles). Form a circle and knit 1st rnd.
2nd rnd: * K2, yfd, k2 tog tbl; rep from * to end.
3rd rnd: * K2 tog, yfd, k2; rep from * to end.
4th to 9th rnd: Rep 2nd and 3rd rnds 3 times.
10th rnd: * K2, yrn twice, k2 tog tbl; rep from * to end.
11th rnd: Knit once into each "yrn twice" of previous rnd, * k2 tog, yrn twice, k2; rep from * to end.
12th to 17th rnd: Rep 10th and 11th rnds 3 times.
18th rnd: * K2, yrn 3 times, k2 tog tbl; rep from * to end.
19th rnd: Knit once into each "yrn 3 times" of previous rnd, * k2 tog, yrn 3 times, k2; rep from * to end.
20th to 24th rnd: Rep 18th and 19th rnds twice, then 18th rnd once.
25th rnd: * K2 tog, work 9 sts into each "yrn 3 times" of previous rnd as follows: k1, (p1, k1) 4 times, k1: rep from * to end.
26th and alt rnd: Knit.
27th rnd: * Yfd, sl 1, k1, psso, k7, k2 tog; rep from * to end.
29th rnd: * Yfd, k1, yfd, sl 1, k1, psso, k5, k2 tog; rep from * to end.
Divide sts onto 7 needles.
31st rnd: * Yfd, k3, yfd, sl 1, k1, psso, k3, k2 tog; rep from * to end.
33rd rnd * Yfd, k5, yfd, sl 1, k1, psso, k1, k2 tog; rep from * to end.

35th rnd: * Yfd, k2, k2 tog, yfd, k3, yfd, sl 1, k2 tog, psso; rep from * to end.
37th rnd: * K4, yfd, k1, yfd, k5; rep from * to end.
39th rnd: * K2, k2 tog, yfd, k3, yfd, sl 1, k1, psso, k3; rep from * to end.
41st rnd: * K1, k2 tog, yfd, k5, yfd, sl 1, k1, psso, k2; rep from * to end.
43rd rnd: * K2 tog, yfd, k3, yfd, k1, yfd, k3, yfd, sl 1, k1, psso, k1; rep from * to end.
45th rnd: Transfer 1 st from left to right and mark new beg of rnd. Adjust sts on other needles as well. * Yfd, k4, yfd, k3, yfd, k4, yfd, sl 1, k2 tog, psso; rep from * to end.
47th rnd: * Yfd, (k5, yfd) 3 times, k1 tbl; rep from * to end.
49th rnd: * Sl 1, k1, psso, k4, yfd, k7, yfd, k4, k2 tog, yfd, k1 tbl, yfd; rep from * to end.
51st rnd: * Sl 1, k1, psso, k3, yfd, k3, k2 tog, yfd, k4, yfd, k3, k2 tog, yfd, sl 1, k2 tog, psso, yfd; rep from * to end.
53rd rnd: * Sl 1, k1, psso, k5, k2 tog, yfd, m2, yfd, sl 1, k1, psso, k5, k2 tog, yfd, sl 1, k2 tog, psso, yfd; rep from * to end.
55th rnd: * Sl 1, k1, psso, k3, k2 tog, yfd, k5, yfd, sl 1, k1, psso, k3, k2 tog, yfd, sl 1, k2 tog, psso, yfd; rep from * to end.
57th rnd: * Sl 1, k1, psso, k1, k2 tog, yfd, k2, yfd, (k1, yfd) 3 times, k2, yfd, sl 1, k1, psso, k1, k2 tog, yfd, sl 1, k2 tog, psso, yfd; rep from * to end.
58th rnd: Knit.

Crochet sts off as follows: * 1 dc into next 3 sts, 10 ch, 1 dc into next 4 sts, 10 ch, 1 dc into next 5 sts, 10 ch, 1 dc into next 4 sts, 10 ch, (1 dc into next 3 sts, 10 ch) twice; rep from * to end, 1 ss in 1st dc.

Cut yarn and work in yarn end.

Fold doily in half lengthwise, with right sides facing, and sew up the opening in the centre, matching pattern carefully. Cut yarn and work in yarn end. Damp, pin out to size and leave to dry.

Table runner

Materials

2 × 50 g Tridalia crochet cotton no. 5
5 double-pointed 2,50 mm knitting needles: 30 cm long
2,50 mm circular knitting needle: 80 cm long
2,00 mm crochet hook

Size: 45 cm × 75 cm

Abbreviations: cr2 – cross 2 stitches = knit into front of 2nd st, knit into front of 1st st, sl both sts off;
m1 – make 1 st = knit into front and back of next st

Instructions

Cast on 162 sts, divide onto 4 needles (1, 80, 1, 80) and form a circle.

Instructions are given for one half of the runner (1st (short) side and 2nd (long) side). Knit the 3rd and 4th sides in the same manner. The number of sts in each side is indicated in brackets.

1st rnd: *1st side:* (K1, p1) twice in st (= 4 sts).
2nd side: M1, (k4, k3 tog, yfd, k2 tbl, yfd, m1, k1 tbl, sl 1, k1, psso, yrn twice, k2 tog, k1 tbl, m1, yfd, k2 tbl, yfd, sl 1, k2 tog, psso, k4) 3 times, m1 (= 88 sts).
2nd and every alt rnd: Knit, but knit tbl all sts worked tbl in previous rnd. K1, p1 in each "yrn twice" of previous rnd.
3rd rnd: *1st side:* M1, k2, m1 (= 6 sts).
2nd side: M1, k1, (k3, k3 tog, yfd, m1, k1 tbl, [sl 1, k1, psso, yrn twice, k2 tog] 3 times, k1 tbl, m1, yfd, sl 1, k2 tog, psso, k3) 3 times, k1, m1 (= 90 sts).
5th rnd: *1st side:* Yrn twice, k1 tbl, k4, k1 tbl (= 8 sts).
2nd side: Yrn twice, k3, (k2, k2 tog, yfd, [sl 1, k1, psso, yrn twice, k2 tog] 5 times, yfd, sl 1, k1, psso, k2) 3 times, k3 (= 92 sts).

Transfer 1 st from left to right at the beg of every alt rnd from the 7th to 51st rnd. Mark new beg of rnd. When sts are transferred at the beg of a rnd, remember to adjust sts on other needles as well.

7th rnd: *1st side:* Yrn twice, m1, yfd, sl 1, k1, psso, k1, * k1, k2 tog, yfd, m1 (= 12 sts).
2nd side: As 1st side to *, (k1, k2 tog, yfd, sl 1, k2 tog, psso, [yrn twice, k2 tog, sl 1, k1, psso] 4 times, yrn twice, k3 tog, yfd, sl 1, k1, psso, k1) 3 times, as 1st side from * to end (= 90 sts).
9th rnd: *1st side:* Yrn twice, sl 1, k1, psso, yrn twice, k2 tog, yfd, sl 1, k1, psso, * k2 tog, yfd, sl 1, k1, psso, yrn twice, k2 tog (= 14 sts).
2nd side: As 1st side to *, (k2 tog, yfd, sl 1, k2 tog, psso, [yrn twice, k2 tog, sl 1, k1, psso] 4 times, yrn twice, k3 tog, yfd,

sl 1, k1, psso) 3 times, as 1st side from * to end (= 86 sts).
11th rnd: *1st side:* Yrn twice, sl 1, k2 tog, psso, yrn twice, k3 tog, yfd, cr2, * yfd, sl 1, k2 tog, psso, yrn twice, k3 tog.
2nd side: As 1st side to *, (yfd, sl 1, k2 tog, psso, [yrn twice, k2 tog, sl 1, k1, psso] 4 times, yrn twice, k3 tog, yfd, cr2) 3 times, as 1st side from * to end.
13th rnd: *1st side:* Yrn twice, m1, yfd, sl 1, k1, psso, yrn twice, k3 tog, yfd, k1 tbl, yrn twice, k1 tbl, * yfd, sl 1, k2 tog, psso, yrn twice, k2 tog, yfd, m1 (= 22 sts).
2nd side: As 1st side to *, (yfd, sl 1, k2 tog, psso, [yrn twice, k2 tog, sl 1, k1, psso] 4 times, yrn twice, k3 tog, yfd, k1 tbl, yrn twice, k1 tbl) 3 times, as 1st side from * to end (= 100 sts).
15th rnd: *1st side:* Yrn twice, sl 1, k1, psso, yrn twice, k2 tog, sl 1, k1, psso, yrn twice, k3 tog, yfd, sl 1, k1, psso, yrn twice, k2 tog, yfd, * sl 1, k2 tog, psso, yrn twice, k2 tog, sl 1, k1, psso, yrn twice, k2 tog (= 24 sts).
2nd side: As 1st side to *, (sl 1, k2 tog, psso, [yrn twice, k2 tog, sl 1, k1, psso] 4 times, yrn twice, k3 tog, yfd, sl 1, k1, psso, k2 tog, yfd) 3 times, as 1st side from * to end (= 102 sts).
17th rnd: *1st side:* Yrn twice, sl 1, k2 tog, psso, yrn twice, k2 tog, sl 1, k1, psso, yrn twice, k2 tog, yfd, k1, sl 1, k1, psso, yrn twice, k2 tog, k1, yfd, * sl 1, k1, psso, yrn twice, k2 tog, sl 1, k1, psso, yrn twice, k3 tog (= 26 sts).
2nd side: As 1st side to *, ([sl 1, k1, psso, yrn twice, k2 tog] 5 times, yfd, k1, sl 1, k1, psso, yrn twice, k2 tog, k1, yfd) 3 times, as 1st side from * to end (= 110 sts).
19th rnd: *1st side:* Yrn twice, m1, yfd, sl 1, k1, psso, yrn twice, k2 tog, sl 1, k1, psso, yfd, k2 tog, yfd, k2, sl 1, k1, psso, yrn twice, k2 tog, k2, yfd, * sl 1, k1, psso, yfd, k2 tog, sl 1, k1, psso, yrn twice, k2 tog, yfd, m1 (= 32 sts).
2nd side: As 1st side to *, (sl 1, k1, psso, yfd, k2 tog, [sl 1, k1, psso, yrn twice, k2 tog] 3 times, sl 1, k1, psso, yfd, k2 tog, yfd, k2, sl 1, k1, psso, yrn twice, k2 tog, k2, yfd) 3 times, as 1st side from * to end (= 116 sts).
21st rnd: *1st side:* Yrn twice, (sl 1, k1, psso, yrn twice, k2 tog) twice, sl 1, k2 tog, psso, yfd, k3, sl 1, k1, psso, yrn twice, k2 tog, k3, yfd, * sl 1, k2 tog, psso, (sl 1, k1, psso, yrn twice, k2 tog) twice (= 32 sts).
2nd side: As 1st side to *, (sl 1, k2 tog, psso, [sl 1, k1, psso, yrn twice, k2 tog] 3 times, sl 1, k2 tog, psso, yfd, k3, sl 1, k1, psso, yrn twice, k2 tog, k3, yfd) 3 times, as 1st side from * to end (= 110 sts).
23rd rnd: *1st side:* Yrn twice, m1, yfd, sl 1, k1, psso, yrn twice, k2 tog, sl 1, k1, psso, yrn twice, k3 tog, yfd, sl 1, k1, psso, k2, yfd, sl 1, k1, psso, yfd, k2 tog, yfd, k2, k2 tog, yfd, * sl 1, k2 tog, psso, yrn twice, k2 tog, sl 1, k1, psso, yrn twice, k2 tog, yfd, m1 (= 37 sts).
2nd side: As 1st side to *, (sl 1, k2 tog, psso, [yrn twice, k2

tog, sl 1, k1, psso] twice, yrn twice, k3 tog, yfd, sl 1, k1, psso, k2, yfd, sl 1, k1, psso, yfd, k2 tog, yfd, k2, k2 tog, yfd) 3 times, as 1st side from * to end (= 112 sts).

25th rnd: *1st side:* Yrn twice, k1 tbl, yfd, k1, * yfd, k2 tog, sl 1, k1, psso, yrn twice, k2 tog, sl 1, k1, psso, yfd, k2 tog, yfd, k1 tbl, yfd, sl 1, k1, psso, k2, yfd, sl 1, k2 tog, psso, yfd, k2, k2 tog, yfd, k1 tbl, yfd, sl 1, k1, psso, ** yfd, k2 tog, sl 1, k1, psso, yrn twice, k2 tog, sl 1, k1, psso, yfd, k1, yfd, k1 tbl (= 41 sts).
2nd side: As 1st side to *; rep 4 times from * to **, and from ** to end (= 116 sts).

27th rnd: *1st side:* Yrn twice, k3, yfd, * sl 1, k2 tog, psso, sl 1, k1, psso, yrn twice, k2 tog, sl 1, k2 tog, psso, yfd, k3, yfd, sl 1, k1, psso, k5, k2 tog, yfd, k3, yfd, ** sl 1, k2 tog, psso, sl 1, k1, psso, yrn twice, k2 tog, sl 1, k2 tog, psso, yfd, k3 (= 39 sts).
2nd side: As 1st side to *; rep 4 times from * to **, and from ** to end (= 108 sts).

29th rnd: *1st side:* Yrn twice, k1 tbl, yfd, sl 1, k2 tog, psso, yfd, k1 tbl, yfd, * sl 1, k2 tog, psso, yrn twice, k3 tog, yfd, k1 tbl, yfd, sl 1, k2 tog, psso, yfd, k1 tbl, yfd, sl 1, k1, psso, k3, k2 tog, yfd, k1 tbl, yfd, sl 1, k2 tog, psso, yfd, k1 tbl, yfd, ** sl 1, k2 tog, psso, yrn twice, k3 tog, yfd, k1 tbl, yfd, sl 1, k2 tog, psso, yfd, k1 tbl (= 41 sts).
2nd side: As 1st side to *; rep 4 times from * to **, and from ** to end (= 110 sts).

31st rnd: *1st side:* Yrn twice, k2, yfd, k3, yfd, k2 tog tbl, yfd, * sl 1, k1, psso, yfd, k2 tog, yfd, k2 tog tbl, yfd, k3, yfd, k2 tog tbl, yfd, sl 1, k1, psso, k1, k2 tog, yfd, k2 tog tbl, yfd, k3, yfd, k2 tog tbl, yfd, ** sl 1, k1, psso, yfd, k2 tog, yfd, k2 tog tbl, yfd, k3, yfd, k2 (= 47 sts).
2nd side: As 1st side to *; rep 4 times from * to **, and from ** to end (= 119 sts).

33rd rnd: *1st side:* Yrn twice, k1 tbl, * yfd, k3, yfd, sl 1, k2 tog, psso; rep from * to last 4 sts, yfd, k3, yfd, k1 tbl (= 51 sts).
2nd side: As 1st side (= 123 sts).

35th rnd: *1st side:* Yrn twice, * k3, yfd, sl 1, k2 tog, psso, yfd; rep from * to last 3 sts, k3 (= 53 sts).
2nd side: As 1st side (= 125 sts).

37th rnd: *1st side:* Yrn twice, k1 tbl, * yfd, sl 1, k2 tog, psso, yfd, k3; rep from * to last 4 sts, yfd, sl 1, k2 tog, psso, yfd, k1 tbl (= 55 sts).
2nd side: As 1st side (= 127 sts).

39th rnd: *1st side:* Yrn twice, k2, * yfd, k3, yfd, sl 1, k2 tog, psso; rep from * to last 5 sts, yfd, k3, yfd, k2 (= 59 sts).
2nd side: As 1st side (= 131 sts).
Change to circular needle and mark beg of rnds and sides.
41st rnd: As 33rd rnd (= 63 sts, 135 sts).
43rd rnd: As 35th rnd (= 65 sts, 137 sts).
45th rnd: *1st side:* Yrn twice, k1 tbl, * (yfd, sl 1, k2 tog, psso, yfd, k3) 3 times, yfd, sl 1, cr2, psso, yfd, k3 **; rep once from * to **, (yfd, sl 1, k2 tog, psso, yfd, k3) twice, yfd, sl 1, k2 tog, psso, yfd, k1 tbl (= 69 sts).
2nd side: As 1st side to *; rep 5 times from * to **, and from ** to end (= 144 sts).

47th rnd: *1st side:* Yrn twice, k2, * (yfd, k3, yfd, sl 1, k2 tog, psso) 3 times, yfd, k4, yfd, sl 1, k2 tog, psso **; rep once from * to **, *** (yfd, k3, yfd, sl 1, k2 tog, psso) twice, yfd, k3, yfd, k2 (= 73 sts).
2nd side: As 1st side to *; rep 5 times from * to **, and from *** to end (= 148 sts).

49th rnd: *1st side:* Yrn twice, k1 tbl, * (yfd, k3, yfd, sl 1, k2 tog, psso) 3 times, yfd, k3, yfd, k4 **; rep once from * to **, *** (yfd, k3, yfd, sl 1, k2 tog, psso) 3 times, yfd, k3, yfd, k1 tbl (= 81 sts).
2nd side: As 1st side to *; rep 5 times from * to **, and from *** to end (= 162 sts).

51st rnd: *1st side:* K1 tbl, yfd, k2, * (yfd, sl 1, k2 tog, psso, yfd, k3) 3 times, yfd, sl 1, k2 tog, psso, yfd, k1, k2 tog, sl 1, k1, psso, k1 **; rep once from * to **, *** (yfd, sl 1, k2 tog, psso, yfd, k3) 3 times, yfd, sl 1, k2 tog, psso, yfd, k2, yfd, k1 tbl (= 79 sts).
2nd side: As 1st side to *; rep 5 times from * to **, and from *** to end (= 154 sts).
Beg following rnds without transferring 1 st from left to right.

53rd rnd: *1st side:* Sl 1, k1, psso, yfd, * sl 1, k1, psso, k1, yfd, sl 1, k1, psso, (yfd, sl 1, k2 tog, psso, yfd, k3) twice, yfd, sl 1, k2 tog, psso, yfd, k2 tog, yfd, k1, k2 tog **; rep twice from * to **, *** yfd, k2 tog (= 73 sts).
2nd side: As 1st side to *; rep 6 times from * to **, and from *** to end (= 142 sts).

55th rnd: *1st side:* Sl 1, k1, psso, yrn twice, * sl 1, k1, psso, k1, (yfd, sl 1, k1, psso) twice, yfd, sl 1, k2 tog, psso, yfd, k3, yfd, sl 1, k2 tog, psso, (yfd, k2 tog) twice, yfd, k1, k2 tog, yrn twice **; rep twice from * to **, k2 tog (= 73 sts).
2nd side: As 1st side to *; rep 6 times from * to **, k2 tog (= 142 sts).

57th rnd: *1st side:* Sl 1, k1, psso, yrn twice, m1, yfd, * sl 1, k1, psso, k1, (yfd, sl 1, k1, psso) 3 times, yfd, sl 1, k2 tog, psso, (yfd, k2 tog) 3 times, yfd, k1, k2 tog, ** yfd, k2 tbl, yfd ***; rep once from * to ***, and once from * to **, yfd, m1, yrn twice, k2 tog (= 77 sts).
2nd side: As 1st side to *; rep 5 times from * to ***, and once from * to **, yfd, m1, yrn twice, k2 tog (= 146 sts).

59th rnd: *1st side:* Sl 1, k1, psso, yrn twice, k2 tog, * sl 1, k1, psso, yfd, sl 1, k1, psso, k1, (yfd, sl 1, k1, psso) 3 times, k1, (k2 tog, yfd) 3 times, k1, k2 tog, yfd, k2 tog **; rep twice from * to **, *** sl 1, k1, psso, yrn twice, k2 tog (= 71 sts).
2nd side: As 1st side to *; rep 6 times from * to **, and from *** to end (= 134 sts).

61st rnd: *1st side:* Sl 1, k1, psso, yrn twice, k2 tog, * sl 1, k1, psso, yfd, sl 1, k1, psso, k1, (yfd, sl 1, k1, psso) twice, yfd, sl 1, k2 tog, psso, (yfd, k2 tog) twice, yfd, k1, k2 tog, yfd, k2 tog **; rep twice from * to **, *** sl 1, k1, psso, yrn twice, k2 tog (= 65 sts).
2nd side: As 1st side to *; rep 6 times from * to **, and from *** to end (= 122 sts).

63rd rnd: *1st side:* Sl 1, k1, psso, yrn twice, k2 tog, * sl 1, k1, psso, yrn twice, sl 1, k1, psso, k1, (yfd, sl 1, k1, psso) twice, k1, (k2 tog, yfd) twice, k1, k2 tog, yrn twice, k2 tog **;

rep twice from * to **, *** sl 1, k1, psso, yrn twice, k2 tog (= 65 sts).

2nd side: As 1st side to *; rep 6 times from * to **, and from *** to end (= 122 sts).

65th rnd: *1st side:* K1 tbl, yrn twice, m1, yrn twice, k2 tog, * sl 1, k1, psso, yrn twice, m1, yfd, sl 1, k1, psso, k1, yfd, sl 1, k1, psso, yfd, sl 1, k2 tog, psso, yfd, k2 tog, yfd, k1, k2 tog, yfd, m1, yrn twice, k2 tog **; rep twice from * to **, *** sl 1, k1, psso, yrn twice, m1, yrn twice, k1 tbl (= 85 sts).

2nd side: As 1st side to *; rep 6 times from * to **, and from *** to end (= 154 sts).

67th rnd: *1st side:* (Sl 1, k1, psso, yrn twice, k2 tog) twice, * sl 1, k1, psso, yrn twice, k2 tog, sl 1, k1, psso, yfd, sl 1, k1, psso, k1, yfd, sl 1, k1, psso, k1, k2 tog, yfd, k1, k2 tog, yfd, k2 tog, sl 1, k1, psso, yrn twice, k2 tog **; rep twice from * to **, *** (sl 1, k1, psso, yrn twice, k2 tog) twice (= 79 sts).

2nd side: As 1st side to *; rep 6 times from * to **, and from *** to end (= 142 sts).

69th rnd: *1st side:* (Sl 1, k1, psso, yrn twice, k2 tog) twice, * sl 1, k1, psso, yrn twice, k2 tog, sl 1, k1, psso, yfd, sl 1, k1, psso, k1, yfd, sl 1, k2 tog, psso, yfd, k1, k2 tog, yfd, k2 tog, sl 1, k1, psso, yrn twice, k2 tog **; rep twice from * to **, *** (sl 1, k1, psso, yrn twice, k2 tog) twice (= 73 sts).

2nd side: As 1st side to *; rep 6 times from * to **, and from *** to end (= 130 sts).

71st rnd: *1st side:* Yfd, sl 1, k1, psso, yrn twice, k2 tog, * (yfd, sl 1, k1, psso, yrn twice, k2 tog) twice, (yfd, sl 1, k1, psso) twice, k3, k2 tog, yfd, k2 tog **; rep twice from * to **, *** (yfd, sl 1, k1, psso, yrn twice, k2 tog) 3 times (= 80 sts).

2nd side: As 1st side to *; rep 6 times from * to **, and from *** to end (= 140 sts).

73rd rnd: *1st side:* Yfd, k1, yfd, sl 1, k1, psso, * (yfd, k2 tog, yfd, k1, yfd, sl 1, k1, psso) 3 times, yfd, sl 1, k1, psso, k1, k2 tog **; rep twice from * to **, *** (yfd, k2 tog, yfd, k1, yfd, sl 1, k1, psso) 3 times, yfd, k2 tog (= 90 sts).

2nd side: As 1st side to *; rep 6 times from * to **, and from *** to end (= 156 sts).

74th rnd: Knit.

Crochet sts off as follows: *1st side:* (1 dc into next 3 sts, 8 ch) 7 times, * (1 dc into next 2 sts, 8 ch, 1 dc into next 3 sts, 8 ch) twice, (1 dc into next 3 sts, 8 ch) 4 times **; rep twice from * to **, 1 dc into next 3 sts, 8 ch. This completes one short side.

2nd side: (1 dc into next 3 sts, 8 ch) 7 times, * (1 dc into next 2 sts, 8 ch, 1 dc into next 3 sts, 8 ch) twice, (1 dc into next 3 sts, 8 ch) 4 times **; rep 5 times from * to **, 1 dc into next 3 sts, 8 ch.

Complete remaining 2 sides in the same manner and finish with 1 ss into 1st dc.

Cut yarn and work in yarn end.

Fold runner in half lengthwise, with right sides facing, and sew up opening in the centre, matching pattern carefully. Cut yarn and work in yarn end. Damp, pin out to size and leave to dry.

Square motif for tablecloth or bedspread

Materials

20 × 50 g Tridalia crochet cotton no. 5 (for tablecloth: 122 cm × 190 cm [77 motifs])
5 double-pointed 2,50 mm knitting needles: 30 cm long
1,75 mm crochet hook

Size: 1 square: 16 cm × 16 cm

Instructions

Cast on 8 sts and divide onto 3 needles (4, 2, 2). Form a circle and knit 4 rnds.
The total number of sts in each rnd is given in brackets at the end of each rnd.
5th rnd: * K1, yfd, k2, yfd, k1; rep from * to end.
6th rnd: * K1, knit 10 sts into next st as follows: (k1, p1) 5 times into the same st, k1; rep from * to end (= 48 sts).
7th rnd: Divide sts onto 4 needles (12 sts on each needle). Using 5th needle, knit to end.
8th rnd: Knit.
9th rnd: * Yfd, k12; rep from * to end.
10th and every alt rnd: Knit.
11th rnd: * Yfd, k1, yfd, k12; rep from * to end (= 60 sts).
13th rnd: * Yfd, k3, yfd, k12; rep from * to end (= 68 sts).
15th rnd: * Yfd, k2, yfd, k1, yfd, k2, yfd, sl 1, k1, psso, k8, k2 tog; rep from * to end (= 76 sts).
17th rnd: * (Yfd, k3) 3 times, yfd, sl 1, k1, psso, k6, k2 tog; rep from * to end (= 84 sts).
19th rnd: * Yfd, k4, yfd, k5, yfd, k4, yfd, sl 1, k1, psso, k4, k2 tog; rep from * to end (= 92 sts).
21st rnd: * Yfd, k5, yfd, k7, yfd, k5, yfd, sl 1, k1, psso, (k2 tog) twice; rep from * to end (= 96 sts).
23rd rnd: * Yfd, k6, yfd, k9, yfd, k6, yfd, sl 1, k2 tog, psso; rep from * to end (= 104 sts).
25th rnd: * Yfd, k25, yfd, k1; rep from * to end (= 112 sts).
27th rnd: * Yfd, k11, k2 tog, yfd, k1, yfd, sl 1, k1, psso, k11, yfd, k1; rep from * to end (= 120 sts)
29th rnd: * Yfd, k11, k2 tog, yfd, k3, yfd, sl 1, k1, psso, k11, yfd, k1; rep from * to end (= 128 sts).

31st rnd: * Yfd, k11, k2 tog, yfd, k5, yfd, sl 1, k1, psso, k11, yfd, k1; rep from * to end (= 136 sts).
33rd rnd: * Yfd, k11, k2 tog, yfd, k7, yfd, sl 1, k1, psso, k11, yfd, k1; rep from * to end (= 144 sts).
34th rnd: Knit.

Cast off loosely. Crochet one rnd of dc around square (1 dc into each st).

Damp, pin out to size and leave to dry. Knit as many squares as required. Sew or crochet squares together neatly, matching pattern carefully. Finish off with a knitted or crocheted border.